M. G. Balme
and M. C. Greenstock

Scrutanda

Oxford University Press

Oxford University Press, Walton Street, Oxford OX2 6DP

OXFORD LONDON GLASGOW
NEW YORK TORONTO MELBOURNE WELLINGTON
KUALA LUMPUR SINGAPORE JAKARTA HONG KONG TOKYO
DELHI BOMBAY CALCUTTA MADRAS KARACHI
IBADAN NAIROBI DAR ES SALAAM CAPE TOWN

First published 1973
Reprinted 1976, 1979

Printed in Great Britain by
Billing & Sons Limited
Guildford and London

Contents

Introduction

Note to the Student

Introduction

This new collection of exercises in comprehension aims at a rather lower level than those in *Intellegenda* (OUP 1970) and can be used by pupils making average progress or at an earlier stage. The exercises are arranged in ascending order of difficulty and the latest are reckoned to be of O-level standard. The collection contains no verse and the prose is adapted, sometimes so drastically that the reference indicates only the original source of the passage.

We have tried to select passages which tell a good story and which give some insight into various aspects of the Roman world. Most are straight-forward narrative and the questions usually demand no more than a simple understanding of the story; but many exercises include one question which requires a grasp of the passage as a whole. The arrangement is by triads, which either tell a continuous story or deal with different aspects of a single theme. Each triad is best read as a whole, and occasionally there is a question after the last of the three pieces that presupposes an understanding of the complete triad.

Some of the triads that tell a continuous story can be used as exercises in rapid reading (e.g. The Flood, Disaster in Gaul); arguments in favour of this practice are offered in the Introduction to *Intellegenda* (pp.xiii–xiv). If they are used in this way, only a selection of the printed questions should be used.

The exercises are equally suitable for oral or written work. We have kept the passages short and have asked a limited number of questions so that any exercise can be completed in a single school period. As we anticipate that written answers will often be required, we have usually asked questions that permit a precise answer. A marking scheme is included that indicates the scale on which the question would be answered. However, we have also included a number of more 'open-ended' questions which require some imagination and insight for good answers; for it seems an important function of such exercises to stimulate these faculties in relation to Latin reading. While unseen translation provides a thorough test of detailed and accurate understanding, comprehension exercises should be a more searching test of deeper under-standing.

The grammar questions are grouped after the questions on content for reasons argued in the Introduction to *Intellegenda* (pp.xiv–xv). A fair amount of help is given with vocabulary (some teachers may think too much—but we have preferred to err on the side of generosity), although we have purposely not given the meaning of some less common words where this can be deduced from the context or from English derivatives.

Harrow-on-the-Hill
July 1973

M.G.B.
M.C.G.

1 The flood

At the beginning of the Iron Age mankind (*genus humanum*) had been extremely wicked.

a. The flood

Iuppiter cum haec vidisset, ira commotus, sic dixit:
'totum genus humanum, quacumque in orbe terrarum
habitat, perdere decrevi. omnia iam temptavi sed
homines in scelere perstant. omnes igitur dabunt poenas
5   quas meruerunt.' et iam fulmina conicere parabat in
omnes terras; sed timuit ne caelum ab ignibus flammas
conciperet. fulmina igitur deposuit atque aliam poenam
sumere decrevit, genus humanum sub undis summergere
et ex omni caelo nimbos demittere. protinus ventum
10 emittit qui nubes nimbosque secum fert. fit fragor.
tum densi funduntur ab aethere nimbi. deinde Iuppiter
Neptunum vocat ut se iuvet. ille fluminum numina
convocat iubetque omnes vires effundere. ipse tridente
suo terram percussit; at illa tremuit et vias aquis
15 patefecit. ruunt flumina per apertos campos; silvas,
homines, domos secum rapiunt. iam mare et terra nullum
discrimen habebant; omnia mare erant.

Ovid, Metamorphoses I, 180ff.

ℓ.1   *haec*: i.e. men's wicked deeds.
ℓ.3   *perdere*: to destroy.
ℓ.4   *perstare*: to persist.
ℓ.5   *merēre* (2): to deserve.   *fulmen, fulminis* (n.): a thunderbolt.
ℓ.9   *nimbus, -i* (m.): a rainstorm.   *protinus* (adv.): straight away.
ℓ.10 *fragor*: a crash of thunder.
ℓ.12 *numen, numinis* (n.): spirit, god.
ℓ.15 *patefacere, patefeci*: to open up.
ℓ.17 *discrimen* (n.): distinction, difference.

(a)   What decision did Jupiter announce in his speech and why had he taken
      this decision?   4

(b)   How did he intend to carry it out at first and why did he change his
      mind?   3

(c)   What did he then decide to do?   1

(d)   How did he start to put his plan into operation?   2

(e)   Whom did he ask to help?   1

(f)   What were the rivers told to do?   2

(g)   What did Neptune do himself and what was the result of his action?   4

(h)   What did the world look like by the end of this passage?   2

(i)   In what case is each of the following: *ira* (ℓ.1); *genus* (ℓ.2); *nimbi* (ℓ.11)? 3

(j)   To whom or what do the following pronouns refer: *se* (ℓ.12);
      ille (ℓ.12); *illa* (ℓ.14)?   3
                                                              _____
                                                              Total 25

b. The survivors

fugiunt homines. hic occupat collem; ille sedet in
cumba et nunc remigat ubi nuper arabat; alter piscem
deprehendit in summa arbore. nat lupus inter oves;
unda vehit leones, unda vehit tigres; aves terra diu
5   quaesita ubi sistere possint, defessae in mare decidunt.
mare colles obruerat undaeque summos montes pulsabant.
omnium hominum qui tunc vivebant optimus erat Deucalion
et iustissimus, uxorque eius, nomine Pyrrha, deos maxime
colebat. illi parva rate vecti ad montem Parnassum
10   incolumes advenerunt ibique ratis adhaesit. rate egressi
primum nymphas et numina montis adorant et Themin, deam
quae tunc oracula tenebat. interim vidit Juppiter totum
orbem terrarum sub undis summersum esse et totum genus
humanum perditum praeter hos duos, qui innocentes erant
15   deosque colebant. nubes igitur dispersit nimbosque removit.
Neptunus quoque aquas aequoris mulcet et flumina revocat.
iam mare litus habet; flumina subsidunt; colles exire
videntur; surgit humus decrescentibus undis.

Ovid, *Metamorphoses* I, 293ff.

ℓ.2   *cumba,-ae:* a boat.   *remigare*: to row.   *piscis, -is*: a fish.
ℓ.3   *nare*: to swim.
ℓ.6   *obruere, obrui*: to overwhelm.
ℓ.9   *ratis, ratis* (f.): a boat.   ℓ.10   *adhaerēre, adhaesi*: to stick, ground.
ℓ.11 *Themin*: Greek acc. of Themis.
ℓ.14 *praeter* (+ acc.): except.
ℓ.16 *mulcēre*: to calm.
ℓ.18 *humus*: the ground.   *decrescere*: to grow smaller, decrease.

(a) Describe three different things which men did when they fled from the flood. 4

(b) What happened to the birds? 3

(c) Why did Jupiter decide to spare Deucalion and Pyrrha? 2

(d) Where did Deucalion and Pyrrha arrive and how did they get there? 2

(e) What did they do as soon as they arrived? 2

(f) How did Jupiter and Neptune put an end to the flood? 4

(g) Describe the steps by which the flood subsided. 4

(h) In what tense are the following verbs:
fugiunt (ℓ.1); *obruerat* (ℓ.6); *pulsabant* (ℓ.6); *adhaesit* (ℓ.10)?
Explain why these different tenses are used. 4

Total 25

c. The oracle

sed Deucalion, postquam terras vidit inanes tacitasque,
lacrimas effudit et sic Pyrrhae dixit: 'nos soli supersumus.
quid faciamus? genus humanum restat in nobis duobus.'
dixerat, et flebant. constituerunt deos precari et auxilium
5   quaerere per sacras sortes. statim igitur templum adeunt.
ubi advenerunt, 'dic, Themis' inquiunt, 'quomodo genus
humanum recreare possimus; fer nobis auxilium.' mota est
dea sortemque dedit: 'discedite templo. velate caput ossaque
magnae parentis post terga iacite.' obstipuerunt diu. tandem
10   Deucalion 'aut ego stultus sum' inquit 'aut magna parens
terra est. lapides enim in corpore terrae sunt ossa. lapides
post terga iacere iubemur.' Pyrrha his verbis mota est.
temptare decernunt. a monte descendunt. velant caput et
lapides post terga iaciunt. lapides lente molliri coeperunt
15   mollitique formam ducere. mox ubi creverunt forma hominum
videri potest. deinde paullatim lapides quos Deucalion
iecerat viri facti sunt, feminae ei quos Pyrrha iecerat. inde
nos homines durum genus sumus et documenta damus qua
origine nati simus.

Ovid, *Metamorphoses* I, 347ff.

ℓ.1   *inanis -e*: empty.
ℓ.2   *superesse*: to survive.
ℓ.5   *sors, sortis* (f.): oracle.
ℓ.8   *velare*: to cover, veil.   *os, ossis* (n.): bone.
ℓ.9   *post terga*: behind (your) backs.
      obstipescere, -stipui: to be dumbfounded.
ℓ.11 *lapis, lapidis* (m.): a stone.
ℓ.14 *molliri*: to grow soft.
ℓ.15 *formam ducere*: to take on a shape.
ℓ.17 *inde*: for this reason.
ℓ.18 *documentum, -i* (n.): proof.

(a) Why did Deucalion weep and what did he say to Pyrrha?   3

(b) What did they decide to do?   2

(c) What did they ask Themis?   2

(d) What did Themis tell them to do?   2

(e) How did Deucalion interpret the oracle?   4

(f) What happened to the stones they threw? List the four stages of change which are described.   5

(g) What, according to Ovid, does this story explain?   2

(h) What has this story in common with the story of Noah?   3

(i) Explain the difference in meaning between *viri* (ℓ.17) and *homines* (ℓ.18).   2

         —————

         Total 25

2 Three stories from early Roman history

These well-known stories were not necessarily accepted as sober history even by those who passed them down: they are more in the nature of folk-tales, like King Alfred and the burnt cakes. Even so, glimpses of historical truth are sometimes seen in them.

a. Population problem

A shortage of women was beginning to cause a decline in Rome's birth-rate, and the neighbouring states would not agree to intermarriage

itaque Romulus ludos Neptuno parat, et finitimas gentes
ad spectaculum invitat. multi homines convenerunt, quod
novam urbem videre studebant: Sabinorum quoque omnis
multitudo venit cum liberis et coniugibus. invitati
5   hospitaliter per domos, cum moenia tectaque plurima
vidissent, mirabantur quod tam brevi tempore Roma crevisset.
ubi spectaculi tempus venit attentaeque eorum mentes cum
oculis erant, tum signo dato iuvenes Romani incurrerunt ut
raperent virgines Sabinas. pleraeque feminae praemium
10   eorum fuerant qui forte ceperant; quasdam, forma excellentes,
primores sibi destinaverant et domos deferebant. primo
mulieres maxime indignabantur: sed Romulus ipse circumibat
dicebatque Romanos eas in matrimonium ducturos esse atque
omnes fortunas communiter habituros. sic animi earum sunt
mitigati.

Livy I, 9.

ℓ.1   *finitimus -a -um*: neighbouring.
ℓ.2   *spectaculum, -i*: a show, games.
ℓ.3   *studēre*: to be eager to.
ℓ.6   *crescere, crevi*: to grow, increase.
ℓ.9   *plerique, pleraeque, pleraque*: very many, most.
         praemium, -i: reward, prize.
ℓ.11   *primores*: leading men.   *destinare*: to pick out.
ℓ.12   *mulier, -eris* (f.): woman.
ℓ.14   *communiter*: in common.

(a) What invitations did Romulus send out, and to whom? 2

(b) Who responded to the invitations? Give as precise details as you can. What was their motive for coming? 4

(c) Describe in your own words the welcome provided by the Romans (ℓℓ. 4–6) and the visitors' reaction to it. 4

(d) For what moment did the young Romans wait before putting their plan into action? 2

(e) What was the plan? 2

(f) Give a free translation of *pleraeque . . . ceperant* (ℓℓ. 9–10). 3

(g) *quasdam* (ℓ.10): what was special about these? Where did they end up? 2

(h) How did the women come to change their minds? What arguments did Romulus use? 4

(i) What evidence can you find in the passage that Rome had been founded only a short time ago? 2

(j) In what cases are the following nouns and why: *Neptuno* (ℓ.1); *moenia* (ℓ.5); *forma* (ℓ.10)? 3

(k) What part of what verb is *ducturos esse* (ℓ.13) and why is this part used? 2

_____

Total 30

13

b. Hard bargaining

anus incognita ad Tarquinium Superbum regem adiit,
novem libros ferens, quos dicebat esse divina oracula:
eos se vendere velle. Tarquinius pretium percontatus est:
mulier nimium atque immensum poposcit. rex, quasi anus
5   aetate desiperet, derisit. tum illa, foculo cum igne coram
rege apposito, tres libros ex novem incendit; et regem
interrogavit num reliquos sex eodem pretio emere vellet.
sed Tarquinius multo magis risit dixitque anum iam sine
dubio delirare. mulier igitur statim tres alios libros
10 incendit; atque rursus placide rogat, ut tres reliquos eodem
illo pretio emat. Tarquinius ore iam serio atque attentiore
animo fit, nam constantiam mulieris confidentiamque videt:
libros tres reliquos emit nihilo minore pretio, quam quod
erat petitum pro omnibus. sed ea mulier tunc a Tarquinio
15 digressa postea nusquam visa est.

Aulus Gellius I, 9.

ℓ.1   *anus, -us* (f.): old woman.
ℓ.3   *percontari*: to inquire.
ℓ.4   *mulier, -eris*: woman.   *nimius -a -um*: excessive.
      poscere, poposci: to demand.   *quasi*: as though.
ℓ.5   *desipere*: to be mad.   *foculus*: brazier of coals.
      coram (+ abl.): in front of.
ℓ.9   *delirare*: to be raving mad.
ℓ.11 *os, oris* (n.): face, expression.
ℓ.14 *petere, -ivi, -itum*: to ask.
ℓ.15 *digredi, -gressus sum*: to depart.   *nusquam*: nowhere.

(a) What did the old woman bring? Give the full name and title of the person to whom she brought them. 3

(b) What did she say about them? 2

(c) Why did Tarquin laugh (ℓ.5)? 3

(d) How did the woman change her offer? 2

(e) What was Tarquin's reaction to this? 2

(f) Was the old woman disturbed by his attitude? Quote a Latin word or phrase to support your answer. 2

(g) Translate *constantia* (ℓ.12) by a word other than 'constancy'. What change did her *constantia* cause in Tarquin's attitude and facial expression? 3

(h) What did he finally do? Explain why he had mixed feelings about the transaction. 3

(i) What details in the story suggest that there was something mysterious about the old woman? 3

(j) Write down two participles from this passage and say with what nouns they agree. 4

(k) Give one English word derived from each of the following: *dicebat* (ℓ.2); *igne* (ℓ.5); *risit* (ℓ.8). 3

Total 30

c. Crisis averted

This incident can be dated to 390 B.C. after the invading Gauls had defeated a Roman army at the river Allia.

interea arx Romae Capitoliumque in ingenti periculo fuit.
nam Galli, humano vestigio notato qua nuntius a Veiis
pervenerat, nocte sublustri praemiserunt inermem qui
temptaret viam. tum, tradentes inter se arma et trahentes
5 alii alios, tanto silentio in summum evaserunt ut non solum
custodes fallerent sed ne canes quidem excitarent. anseres
non fefellerunt, a quibus (nam sacri erant Iunoni) in summa
inopia cibi tamen cives abstinebant. quae res Romanos
servavit: nam clangore eorum alarumque crepitu excitatus
10 M. Manlius, qui triennio ante consul fuerat, vir bello
egregius, armis arreptis Gallum qui iam in summo constiterat
umbone deturbat. iamque et alii, voce illius congregati,
telis saxisque proturbaverunt hostes, totaque acies in
praeceps prolapsa est.

Livy V, 47.

ℓ.2   *vestigium, -i* (n.): footprint, track.
ℓ.3   *sublustris -e*: starlit.   *inermis -e*: unarmed.
ℓ.4   *temptare*: to attempt, explore.   *inter se*: to each other.
ℓ.5   *evadere, evasi*: to come out, emerge.
ℓ.6   *fallere, fefelli* (+ acc.): to escape the notice of.
        excitare: to wake up.   *anser, -eris* (m.): goose.
ℓ.8   *inopia, -ae*: scarcity.
ℓ.9   *clangor, -oris*: noise of cackling.   *crepitus, -us:* noise of beating.
        ala, -ae: wing.
ℓ.10 *triennium, -i:* three years.
ℓ.11 *egregius*: outstanding.
ℓ.12 *umbo, -onis*: boss of shield.   *deturbare*: to send flying.
ℓ.14 *in praeceps:* headlong.

(a)   What was the state of affairs at Rome?   2

(b)   How did the Gauls discover the way to the summit? When did they attempt the ascent?   3

(c)   What evidence do you find of good organization on the ascent?   3

(d)   Explain how the Gauls' attempt to ascend in total silence nearly succeeded, but not quite.   3

(e)   How had the Roman citizens shown great self-restraint with regard to the geese? Why had they done so?   3

(f)   What information are we given about Manlius' previous career?   2

(g)   Basing your account on lines 9–12, write (in English) a paragraph from an imaginary diary of Manlius describing what he heard and saw and did.   5

(h)   Who are the *alii* in line 12? What part did they play in repulsing the invaders?   3

(i)   In what case is each of the following: *ingenti* (ℓ.1); *sacri* (ℓ.7); *Iunoni* (ℓ.7)?   3

(j)   Distinguish between the meanings of these phrases: *in summum* (ℓ.5); *in summa inopia* (ℓℓ.7-8); *in summo* (ℓ.11).   3

Total 30

3   Saint Paul shipwrecked

**Paul was arrested in Jerusalem and was sent in about A.D. 60 to stand trial
before Nero at Rome. On the voyage with him was Luke, who wrote an
account of their experiences.**

a. Gale

*The ship, with 276 people on board, had already encountered strong winds
but had managed to reach a harbour in Crete called Fair Havens.*

cum in hoc portu hiemare non possemus, constituimus
navigare, si possemus, ad Phoinicem et ibi hiemare. et ubi
adspirare coepit Auster, navem solvimus et legebamus Cretam.
haud multo post autem ventus qui vocatur Euroaquilo descendit
5   in nos, et cum non possemus procedere contra ventum, navis
praeceps ferebatur. ubi sub Caudam insulam venimus, primum
magno cum labore scapham sustulimus; deinde, timentes
ne in Syrtim impelleremur, vela summisimus. iam valida
tempestas nos ferebat et iactabat. sequenti die mercis
10   iacturam nautae fecerunt et tertio die suis manibus armamenta
navis proiecerunt. neque autem sole neque sideribus
apparentibus per multos dies, et tempestate maxima instante,
iam ablata est omnis spes salutis nostrae.

The Vulgate, Acts of the Apostles xxviii, 12-20.

ℓ.1   *hiemare*: to spend the winter.
ℓ.3   *adspirare*: to blow (of a favourable wind).   *Auster*: the south wind.
         legere: to sail along the coast of, coast along.
ℓ.4   *Euroaquilo*: the north-east wind.
ℓ.6   *praeceps*: headlong.   *sub*: under the shelter of.
ℓ.7   *scapha, -ae*: ship's dinghy.   *sustulimus*: 'we took on board.'
ℓ.8   *Syrtis*, acc. *Syrtim*: a sandbank on the African coast.
         vela summittere, -misi: to lower sails.
ℓ.9   *iactare*: to toss, throw about.   *merx, mercis* (f.): cargo.
ℓ.10   *iacturam facere* (+ gen.): to throw overboard.
         armamenta, -orum (n. pl.): the ship's tackle (sails, ropes etc.).
ℓ.11   *sidus, -eris*: star.
ℓ.12   *instare*: to press hard upon.

(a) Why did they decide to continue to Phoenix? 2

(b) What weather conditions encouraged them to begin with? 1

(c) What change in the weather then occurred? What result did this have? 3

(d) Describe and explain what they did when they reached the shelter of Cauda. 4

(e) *iam . . . proiecerunt* (ℓℓ.8–11). What was the weather like now? What steps did they take to lighten the ship? 4

(f) Describe the next stage of the journey (*per multos dies*) and the state of mind of those on board. 5

(g) Give the subject of the following verbs, in Latin or English: *coepit* (ℓ.3); *proiecerunt* (ℓ.11); *ablata est* (ℓ.13). 3

(h) In what different ways is the ablative case used in the following words: *die* (ℓ.10); *manibus* (ℓ.10); *sole* (ℓ.11)? 3

Total 25

19

b. Shipwreck

sed ubi quartadecima nox tempestatis venit, circa mediam
noctem nautae suspicabantur se terrae appropinquare;
timentes autem ne in saxa incideremus, de puppi ancoras
quattuor miserunt. cupientes tamen e nave effugere, nautae
5   scapham demittebant in mare, simulantes se ancoras de prora
extendere. at Paulus dixit centurioni et militibus: 'nisi
hi in nave manserint, vos salvi fieri non potestis.' tum
milites absciderunt funes scaphae et passi sunt eam excidere.
cum autem dies factus esset, terram ignotam vidimus:
10   constituerunt igitur navem impellere in litus. tandem navis
in harenam fixa est et vi maris frangebatur. consilium autem
fuit militum custodias interficere ne quis effugeret: centurio
autem volens servare Paulum prohibuit hoc fieri. iussit eos
qui possent natare, emittere se primo et ad terram exire.
15   tum ceteri in tabulis et fractis partibus navis ferebantur.
et sic factum est ut omnes evaderent ad terram.

The Vulgate, Acts of the Apostles xxviii, 17-44.

ℓ.3   *incidere in*: to run on to.   *puppis,* abl. *puppi*: stern.
ℓ.5   *scapha, -ae*: ship's dinghy.   *simulare*: to pretend.
       prora, -ae: prow.
ℓ.7   *salvus -a -um*: safe.
ℓ.8   *abscindere, abscidi*: to cut through.   *funis, -is*: rope.
       excidere: to fall into the water.
ℓ.11   *harena, -ae*: sandbank.   ℓ.12 *custodiae, -arum* (f. pl.): the prisoners.
ℓ.14 *natare:* to swim.
ℓ.15 *tabula, -ae*: plank.
ℓ.16 *evadere:* to escape.

(a) How long had they been sailing since the storm started?　　　　1

(b) What were the sailors afraid of and what steps did they take to
prevent it?　　　　3

(c) How did the sailors then try to save their own skins?　　　　2

(d) How were they prevented?　　　　3

(e) What sight met them at dawn? What decision did they take?　　　　2

(f) Why were the prisoners in danger? How were they saved?　　　　3

(g) Describe the different ways by which everybody finally managed
to get ashore safely.　　　　4

(h) What did the centurion think of Paul? Give two pieces of evidence
from this passage.　　　　2

(i) What groups of people are referred to by the following pronouns:
hi (ℓ.7); *vos* (ℓ.7); *se* (ℓ.14)?　　　　3

(j) What tense of the verb is *manserint* (ℓ.7) and why is this tense used?　2

Total 25

c. Rescue

ubi evasimus in litus, cognovimus Melitam esse nomen
insulae. ibi barbari pyram incenderunt propter imbrem et
frigus, et humanissime nos acceperunt. cum collegisset
autem Paulus sarmenta et imponeret super ignem, vipera
5   propter calorem processit et pendebat de manu eius. quam
ubi viderunt barbari, inter se dicebant: 'certe homicida est
homo hic; nam quamquam evasit e mari, Ultio non sinit
eum vivere.' at ille excussit viperam in ignem et nihil mali
passus est. diu autem illi exspectabant eum subito moriturum
10 esse; sed videntes eum nihil mali pati, sententiam converterunt
et dicebant eum esse deum. princeps autem insulae, nomine
Publius, nos triduo apud se hospitaliter excipiebat. et cum
tandem navigaremus, imposuerunt in navem omnia quae
necessaria erant. et sic venimus Romam.

The Vulgate, Acts of the Apostles xxviii, 1-14.

ℓ.1   *Melita, -ae*: Malta.
ℓ.2   *pyra, -ae*: large fire.
ℓ.4   *sarmenta, -orum* (n. pl.): twigs.   *vipera, -ae* (f.): adder.
ℓ.5   *calor, -oris*: heat.
ℓ.6   *homicida, -ae* (m.): murderer.
ℓ.7   *Ultio*: The Goddess of Vengeance.   *sinere*: to allow.
ℓ.8   *excutere, excussi*: to shake off.   *nihil mali*: 'no harm'.
ℓ.10 *sententia, -ae*: opinion.
ℓ.12 *triduo* (adv.): for three days.   *excipere*: to welcome.

(a) What did they discover when they reached the shore?   1

(b) What were the weather conditions like?   2

(c) What sort of welcome did they receive from the local inhabitants?   2

(d) How did Paul make himself useful?   2

(e) What danger did he find himself in? How did he escape (ℓℓ. 4–9)?   3

(f) *dicebant* (ℓ.6): how did the inhabitants explain what had just happened to Paul?   3

(g) What were they expecting to happen next?   1

(h) *dicebant* (ℓ.11): how and why did they change their minds?   2

(i) What further kindnesses were shown by the *barbari*?   4

(j) Explain why these verbs are in the infinitive:
vivere (ℓ.8); *pati* (ℓ.10).   2

(k) Translate *quam ubi viderunt barbari* (ℓℓ. 5–6) into good English.
To what or whom does *quam* refer?   3

Total 25

4   Three stories from Petronius

The following three stories are taken from the *Cena Trimalchionis*; this is part
of a Latin novel and describes an extraordinary dinner party given by the
millionaire Trimalchio. The first and third passages are stories which Trimalchio
tells his guests; the second passage describes an incident during the dinner.

a. An unlucky inventor

fuit olim faber qui fecit phialam vitream quae frangi non poterat.
voluit igitur eam Caesari dare. admissus est ad Caesarem cum
suo munere. deinde phialam porrigebat Caesari et eam proiecit
in pavimentum. Caesar perterritus est. at ille sustulit phialam
5 de terra; collisa est tamquam vasum aeneum; deinde
martiolum de sinu protulit et phialam facillime correxit.
hoc facto putabat se solium Iovis tenere, utique postquam
Caesar ei dixit: 'num quis alius scit talem phialam facere?'
sed postquam faber negavit, iussit illum Caesar decollari. si enim
10 omnibus scitum esset, aurum pro luto haberemus.

Petronius, *Satyricon* 51.

ℓ.1   *faber*: a craftsman.   *phiala vitrea*: a glass bowl.
ℓ.2   *Caesari*: the emperor.
ℓ.3   *porrigere*: to hold out.
ℓ.5   *collisa est tamquam vasum aeneum*: 'it was dented like a bronze dish'.
ℓ.6   *martiolus, -i* (m.): a little hammer.
ℓ.7   *solium, -i* (n.): throne.   *utique*: especially.
ℓ.9   *decollare*: to behead.
ℓ.10   *pro luto*: as cheap as dirt.

(a)   What did the craftsman invent?   1

(b)   What did he decide to do with his invention?   1

(c)   When he was admitted to Caesar, what did he do with his gift?   2

(d)   Why do you suppose Caesar was frightened?   2

(e)   How did the craftsman repair the bowl?   2

(f)   *putabat se solium Iovis tenere* (ℓ.7): translate (a) literally (b) freely, to show the meaning of this saying.   2

(g)   What did Caesar ask the craftsman?   2

(h)   How did Caesar reward him?   2

(i)   Explain in your own words why he did this.   2

(j)   What tenses are *porrigebat* and *proiecit* (ℓ.3)? Account for the change of tense.   3

(k)   What part of speech is each of the following? If it is a verb say what part of the verb, if a noun or pronoun, say what case it is in: *dare* (ℓ.2); *munere* (ℓ.3); *ille* (ℓ.4); *facillime* (ℓ.6); *se* (ℓ.7); *ei* (ℓ.8).   6

Total 25

b. A dog fight

deinde Trimalchio ad servum respexit quem Croesum
appellabat. Croesus catellae nigrae et indecenter
pingui panem dabat. quo viso Trimalchio Scylacem
iussit adduci 'praesidium domus familiaeque'. sine
5 mora ingens adductus est canis qui ante mensam se
posuit. tum Trimalchio iaciens ei candidum panem 'nemo'
inquit 'in domo mea me plus amat.' iratus Croesus quod
Trimalchio Scylacem tam effuse laudaret, catellam in
terram deposuit hortatusque est ut pugnaret. Scylax
10 ingenti latratu triclinium implevit catellamque Croesi
paene laceravit. nec solum tumultum praebuerunt
canes, sed candelabrum etiam super mensam eversum
et vasa omnia crystallina fregit et oleo ferventi
aliquot convivas respersit. at Trimalchio, ne videretur
15 iactura motus esse, basiavit Croesum et iussit potionem
ei dari.

Petronius, Satyricon 64.

ℓ.2 *catella, -ae*: a puppy.
ℓ.3 *pinguis -e*: fat.
ℓ.10 *latratus, -us*: barking.   *triclinium, -i*: dining-room.
ℓ.11 *praebēre*: to cause.
ℓ.12 *candelabrum, -i* (n.): a lamp-stand.
ℓ.13 *oleo ferventi*: with burning oil.
ℓ.14 *conviva, -ae* (m.): a guest.   *respergere, respersi*: to spatter.
ℓ.15 *iactura, -ae* (f.): loss.   *basiare*: to kiss.
      potio, potionis (f.): a drink.

(a) What was Croesus doing when Trimalchio looked at him?   2

(b) What do you learn about the appearance of Croesus' puppy?   2

(c) How does Trimalchio describe Scylax?   2

(d) Why was Croesus angry?   2

(e) What did he then do with this puppy?   3

(f) What accident occurred in the course of the fight?   4

(g) Why did Trimalchio kiss Croesus?   2

(h) In what ways does the behaviour of Trimalchio seem to you unexpected?   2

(i) What part of the verb is each of the following forms: *adduci* (ℓ.4); *eversum* (ℓ.12); *motus esse* (ℓ.15)?   3

(j) In what case is each of the following words: *pingui* (ℓ.3); *mora* (ℓ.5); *ingenti* (ℓ.10)?   3

Total 25

c. A horror story

cum ego iuvenis essem, puer quidam in domo nostra
mortuus est. dum igitur mater misera eum plangeret
et nos omnes tristes essemus, subito strigae stridere
coeperunt. habebamus tunc servum longum, audacem,
5 validissimum; poterat bovem iratum tollere. hic audacter
stricto gladio extra ostium cucurrit et strigam mediam
traiecit. audivimus gemitum sed strigas ipsas non
vidimus. servus autem reversus se proiecit in lectum
et corpus totum lividum habebat. nos clauso ostio
10 rediimus iterum ad officium. sed dum mater amplectitur
corpus filii sui, tangit et videt manuciolum de stramentis factum. non cor habebat, non intestina, non
quicquam; nam iam puerum strigae surripuerant et
supposuerant stramenticum vavetonem. servus autem ille
15 longus post hoc factum numquam coloris sui fuit sed
post paucos dies phreneticus periit.

Petronius, Satyricon 63.

  ℓ.2 *plangere*: to lament.
  ℓ.3 *striga, -ae* (f.): a witch. *stridere*: to shriek.
  ℓ.5 *bos, bovis* (m.): a bull.
  ℓ.7 *traicere, traieci*: to pierce. *gemitus, -us* (m.): a groan.
  ℓ.8 *lectus, -i* (m.): bed.
  ℓ.9 *lividus -a -um*: black and blue. *ostium, -i* (n.): door.
  ℓ.10 *amplecti*: to embrace.
  ℓℓ.11−12 *manuciolum de stramentis factum*: a bundle made of straw.
  ℓ.12 *cor, cordis* (n.): heart.
  ℓ.14 *supponere, supposui*: to put in place, to substitute.
     vaveto, vavetonem: a dummy.
  ℓ.16 *phreneticus -a -um*: delirious.

(a) What happened while the mother was mourning her son?   1

(b) Describe the slave referred to in ℓ.4. What evidence does
Trimalchio give of his strength?   4

(c) What did the slave do when he heard the witches?   3

(d) What was the matter with him when he came back?   2

(e) What did 'we' do when the slave came back?   2

(f) When the mother embraced her son, what did she see?   1

(g) How does Trimalchio account for what had happened to the body?   2

(h) What happened to the slave?   2

(i) What supernatural powers does Trimalchio attribute to witches?   3

(j) In what case is *gladio* (ℓ.6), and why? Give another example of
this construction from this passage.   2

(k) In what case is each of the following pronouns:
se (ℓ.8); *quicquam* (ℓ.13); *ille* (ℓ.14)?   3

Total 25

5 Disaster in Gaul

A Roman army under the command of Q. Sabinus and L. Cotta was marching
through the forests of Gaul into winter quarters. They had had an offer of safe
conduct through the territory of Ambiorix, an apparently friendly local chieftain.
The passages, which form a continuous narrative, begin as the Romans debated
whether to leave their camp or not.

a. Ambush

Sabinus promissis Ambiorigis confidere vult; Cotta tamen
affirmat se numquam consilium hostis accepturum esse. tandem,
postquam ad mediam noctem disputaverunt, Cotta et ceteri
legati cum Sabino consentiunt. prima luce Romani incaute ex
5   castris proficiscuntur, tamquam non ab hoste sed ab amico
Ambiorige consilium accepissent: nam longissimum habent
agmen cum maximis impedimentis. at hostes, qui ex nocturno
fremitu senserunt Romanos exire, collocaverant insidias
bipertito in silvis a duobus milibus passuum et Romanorum
10   adventum exspectabant. ubi iam maior pars agminis in vallem
descendit, Galli subito ex utraque parte vallis se ostendunt
et novissimos aggredi, primos ascensu prohibere coeperunt.
tum Sabinus, cum nihil antea providisset, trepidat, huc illuc
currit, cohortes instruere conatur. Cotta tamen, qui putaverat
15   haec in itinere posse accidere, omnia faciebat ut suos servaret:
nam et milites cohortabatur et ipse fortiter pugnabat.

Caesar, de Bello Gallico V, 31-3.

ℓ.4   *consentire*: to agree.
ℓ.5   *tamquam* (+ subj.): as though.
ℓ.7   *impedimenta, -orum* (n. pl.): baggage-train.
ℓ.8   *fremitus, -us* (m.): noise, din.   *collocare*: to place, set up.
ℓ.9   *bipertito* (adv.): in two companies.   *a*: at a distance of.
ℓ.11   *se ostendere*: to show, reveal oneself.
ℓ.12   *novissimi, -orum* (m. pl.): the last in the line of march.
ℓ.15   *accidere*: to happen.

(a) What was the main point of disagreement between Sabinus and Cotta? For how long did their argument continue and who eventually won? 4

(b) What accounted for the Romans' lack of caution as they set out at dawn? How was this shown by their formation? 4

(c) Describe the position chosen by the Gauls for their ambush. How had they guessed that the Romans were coming? 3

(d) Describe the Gallic attack from the Roman point of view. Use a sketch-map to make your description clearer, and include the position of the Roman camp. 5

(e) How did Sabinus' behaviour show his lack of foresight? 3

(f) To what does *haec* (ℓ.15) refer? Explain why Cotta was not caught unprepared. 2

(g) Show how Cotta behaved as a good general and soldier should. 3

(h) In what tenses are the following verbs:
collocaverant (ℓ.8); *exspectabant* (ℓ.10); *ostendunt* (ℓ.11)?
Give reasons for the changes of tense. 6

Total 30

b. Resistance

itaque duces Romani iusserunt milites impedimenta
relinquere atque in orbem consistere. hoc consilium tamen
et nostris militibus spem diminuit et hostes ad pugnam
alacriores effecit; credebant enim Romanos summo timore
5   ac desperatione id fecisse. erant et virtute et numero
pares. nostri, quamquam a duce et a fortuna deserebantur,
tamen omnem spem salutis in virtute ponebant, et quotiens
quaeque cohors procurrerat, magnus numerus hostium cadebat.
Ambiorix haec animadvertit et suos iubet tela procul
10 conicere. itaque cum Romani impetum faciunt, recedunt
barbari; cum tamen in locum reverti coeperunt, illi non solum
propius accedunt sed etiam circumveniunt. sin autem Romani
locum tenere vellent, tam conferti erant ut nec singuli
virtutem praestare nec universi multitudinem telorum vitare
15 possent. multis tamen vulneribus acceptis resistebant et
a prima luce ad horam octavam pugnantes nihil indignum
committebant.

Caesar, *de Bello Gallico* V, 33-5.

ℓ.1   *impedimenta, -orum* (n. pl.): baggage.
ℓ.2   *orbis, -is*: a circle.
ℓ.4   *alacer -cris -cre*: keen, eager.
ℓ.5   *ac*: and.
ℓ.6   *par*: equal.
ℓ.7   *quotiens*: as often as.
ℓ.8   *quisque, quaeque, quodque*: each.
ℓ.12 *sin autem*: but if.
ℓ.13 *confertus -a -um*: close-packed.   *singuli*: individuals.
ℓ.14 *praestare*: to display, show.   *vitare*: to avoid.

(a) What orders did Sabinus and Cotta give?   2

(b) What effect did these orders have on the Romans and on the enemy?   2

(c) What did the enemy believe about the Romans' state of mind?   2

(d) What tactics did the surrounded Romans use at first (ℓℓ.7–8)? Were they successful?   3

(e) Why and how did Ambiorix change his plan of attack?   3

(f) Translate the words *recedunt* (ℓ.10) and *accedunt* (ℓ.12). Why did the Gauls do this?   4

(g) What did the Romans find when they tried to stand their ground? How were they at a double disadvantage (marked by *singuli . . . universi* ℓℓ.13–14)?   4

(h) Does the writer (Caesar) praise or blame the Roman cohorts? How long had they been under fire, and how had they behaved?   4

(i) Translate *erant et virtute et numero pares* (ℓℓ.5–6).   3

(j) Say precisely why the following tenses are used: *procurrerat* (ℓ.8); *cadebat* (ℓ.8); *animadvertit* (ℓ.9).   3

Total 30

c. Annihilation

tandem Sabinus constituit ab Ambiorige salutem sibi
militibusque petere. Cotta tamen, qui in adversum os funda
vulneratus erat, negat se ad armatum hostem iturum esse
atque in eo perseverat. Sabinus cum reliquis tribunis
5 militum et primorum ordinum centurionibus Ambiorigi
appropinquat: iussus est arma abicere, suosque idem facere
iubet. inde, dum de condicionibus pacis colloquuntur,
paulatim circumventus interficitur. quo facto hostes
ululatum tollunt impetumque in nostros faciunt. ibi Cotta
10 pugnans interficitur cum maxima parte militum. reliqui se
in castra recipiunt: ex quibus L. Petrosidius aquilifer,
multis hostibus instantibus, aquilam intra vallum proiecit;
ipse pro castris fortissime pugnans occiditur. illi aegre
ad noctem oppugnationem sustinent; noctu desperata salute
15 omnes ad unum se ipsi occidunt. pauci e proelio elapsi
incertis itineribus per silvas ad T. Labienum in hiberna
perveniunt atque eum de rebus gestis certiorem faciunt.

Caesar, *de Bello Gallico* V, 35-7.

ℓ.2   *in adversum os*: full in his face.   *funda, -ae*: a sling-stone.
ℓ.8   *paulatim*: gradually, little by little.
ℓ.9   *ululatus, -us*: war cry.
ℓ.12 *instare*: to attack relentlessly.
ℓ.13 *aegre* (adv.): with difficulty.
ℓ.14 *sustinēre*: to resist, fight off.
ℓ.15 *ad unum*: to a man, without exception.   *elabi, elapsus sum*: to escape.
ℓ.16 *hiberna, -orum* (n. pl.): winter quarters.

(a) What decision did Sabinus finally take?   2

(b) Why did Cotta disagree with him?   1

(c) Describe the parley with Ambiorix and how it ended (ℓℓ.4–9).   6

(d) Give evidence of Petrosidius' loyalty and bravery.   3

(e) Who are referred to by *illi* (ℓ.13)? What did they do during the
     night? Why?   4

(f) How did Labienus (one of Caesar's generals) hear about these
     events?
                                                                                            3

(g) What can you find out about Cotta's character from this passage?   3

(h) (For those who have studied all three passages.)
     nostri . . . a duce et a fortuna deserebantur (passage b line 6):
     do you consider this to be a fair verdict on the disaster as a whole?   3

(i) Translate *circumventus* (ℓ.8) and *elapsi* (ℓ.15). Which of them is
     a deponent verb and what difference does this make to its
     meaning?   3

(j) Write down in Latin an ablative absolute phrase from this passage
     and translate it.   2
                                                                                  _____
                                                                                   Total 30

6   The old virtues

The following three stories illustrate the grand old Roman virtues of *pietas*
(sense of duty towards gods, family, and country), *fides* (trustworthiness),
and *pudicitia* (chastity). Livy and his contemporaries often lament the rarity
of these virtues in their own time.

a. Pietas

*Coriolanus, a Roman, had joined the enemies of Rome and was about to lead
them in an attack on the city.*

cum hostes de pace agere nollent, matronae ad Veturiam
matrem Coriolani Volumniamque uxorem frequentes coeunt.
constituerunt in castra hostium ire, ut urbem, quam
armis viri non defendere possent, mulieres precibus
5   lacrimisque defenderent. ubi ad castra venerunt et
nuntiatum est Coriolano adesse ingens agmen mulierum,
primum cognoscere noluit quae vellent. deinde amicorum
quidam 'nisi me fallunt oculi' inquit 'mater tua et
coniunx adsunt.' cum Coriolanus consternatus a sede
10 sua cucurrisset ut matrem salutaret, mulier in iram
a precibus versa 'dic mihi' inquit 'utrum ad hostem
an ad filium venerim, utrum captiva an mater in castris
tuis sim.' ille penitus commotus est. matrem uxoremque
complexus dimittit; ipse ab urbe castra movit. abductis
15 inde legionibus ex agro Romano, paullo post mortuus est.

Livy II, 40.

ℓ.1   *agere de*: to discuss.
ℓ.2   *frequentes*: in crowds.
ℓ.4   *preces, precum* (f. pl.): prayers.
ℓ.8   *fallere*: to deceive.
ℓ.13 *penitus* (adv.): deeply.
ℓ.14 *complecti, complexus sum*: to embrace.
ℓ.15 *ager Romanus*: Roman territory.

(a) Who were Veturia and Volumnia? Why did the *matronae* come
to them?   3

(b) What did they decide to do? With which Latin words are
armis and *viri* (ℓ.4) contrasted?   3

(c) What was the first report Coriolanus heard about the action taken
by Veturia and Volumnia?   2

(d) What was his first reaction?   2

(e) Who gave him further information? What was it?   3

(f) What did Coriolanus do when he received this information? Why
did he do this?   2

(g) How did his mother react? What did she say?   4

(h) What effect did Veturia's words have on Coriolanus? What did he
do and what happened to him in the end?   4

(i) What aspects of *pietas* are illustrated in this story?   3

(j) What part of the verb is each of the following forms and why is
this part used: *adesse* (ℓ.6); *vellent* (ℓ.7); *dic* (ℓ.11); *venerim* (ℓ.12)?   4

                                                          _____
                                                          Total 30

b. Fides

The town of Falerii is being besieged by the Romans.

magister, qui filios principum Faleriis erudiebat, cum
in pace instituisset pueros ante urbem producere ut
se exercerent, eum morem per belli tempus non intermisit
sed modo brevioribus modo longioribus spatiis
5 trahebat eos a porta. postremo longius solito
progressus eos inter stationes Romanorum in castra
ad Camillum perduxit. ibi scelesto facinori scelestiorem
sermonem addidit; dixit enim se Falerios in manus
Romanorum tradidisse, cum filios principum in potestatem
10 eorum dedidisset. quae ubi Camillus audivit, 'non est
similis tui' inquit 'nec populus nec imperator ad quos
scelestus ipse cum scelesto munere venisti. sunt et belli,
sicut pacis, iura. arma habemus non adversus pueros sed
adversus armatos, qui Romanos nec laesi nec lacessiti
15 oppugnaverunt.' denudatum deinde eum, manibus post
tergum vinctis, pueris tradidit ut Falerios reducerent
virgasque quibus proditorem agerent in urbem eis dedit.

Livy V, 27.

ℓ.1   *princeps, principis* (m.): a leading man, chief.
      erudire: to train, educate.
ℓ.2   *instituere, -tui, -tutum*: to set up, begin.
ℓ.4   *modo . . . modo . . .*: now . . . now. . .
ℓ.5   *solito* (abl.): than usual.
ℓ.6   *statio, stationis*: outpost, picket.
ℓ.7   *scelestus -a -um*: wicked, criminal.   *facinus, facinoris* (n.): deed.
ℓ.11 *similis -e* (+ gen.): like, similar to.
ℓ.13 *sicut*: as.
ℓ.14 *lacessere, -ivi, -itum*: to provoke.   ℓ.15 *denudare*: to strip.
ℓ.17 *virga, -ae*: stick, rod.

(a) What was the schoolmaster's special job? 1

(b) What routine had he begun before the war? 2

(c) When war began, in what way was his conduct suspicious? 2

(d) Draw a plan to illustrate the meaning of the sentence *postremo . . . perduxit*(ℓℓ. 5–7). Label the key features in Latin. 3

(e) What did the schoolmaster say in his *scelestus sermo*? 3

(f) In his reply how does Camillus condemn the conduct of (i) the schoolmaster (ii) the people of Falerii? 3

(g) What did Camillus do to the schoolmaster? 4

(h) Livy ends this story by saying: *fides Romana, iustitia imperatoris in foro et in curia* (senate house) *celebrantur.* What does Livy mean by *fides Romana* and how does the story illustrate it? 4

(i) In what cases are *Faleriis* (ℓ.1) and *Falerios* (ℓ.16) and why are these cases used? 2

(j) Why is *agerent* (ℓ.17) in the subjunctive mood? 1

———————
Total 25

c. Pudicitia

Sextus Tarquinius had first met Lucretia shortly before the events described in this passage. She was the wife of a fellow officer in the army and they had ridden over from camp to visit her at Collatia.

paucis post diebus Sextus Tarquinius cum comite uno
Collatiam venit. ibi exceptus benigne post cenam in
hospitale cubiculum deductus est. deinde amore ardens,
postquam satis tuta omnia videbantur sopitique omnes,
5   stricto gladio ad dormientem Lucretiam venit sinistra-
que manu mulieris pectore oppresso 'tace, Lucretia,'
inquit; 'Sextus Tarquinius sum; ferrum in manu est;
moriere, si emiseris vocem.' cum territa ex somno
mulier nullam opem, prope mortem imminentem videret,
10   tum Tarquinius fatetur amorem, orat, miscet precibus
minas. ubi eam obstinatam videbat et ne mortis quidem
metu inclinari, addit ad metum dedecus: dicit se cum ea
mortua iugulatum servum nudum positurum esse, ut
in sordido adulterio necata esse dicatur. quo terrore
15   cum vicisset obstinatam pudicitiam victrix libido,
profectus est inde Tarquinius ferox expugnato decore
muliebri.

Livy I, 58.

ℓ.3   *hospitale cubiculum*: the guest's bedroom.
ℓ.4   *sopitus -a -um*: sound asleep.
ℓ.9   (*ops*), *opis* (f.): help.   *imminēre*: to threaten, hang over.
ℓ.11   *mina, -ae*: a threat.
ℓ.12   *inclinare*: to sway, influence.
         dedecus, dedecoris (n.): dishonour.
ℓ.13   *iugulare*: to cut the throat of.
ℓ.15   *victrix libido*: victorious lust.
ℓ.16   *expugnare*: to take by storm.

40

(a)   How was Tarquinius received when he arrived at Collatia?   2

(b)   When and in what frame of mind did he set off for Lucretia's room?   3

(c)   Translate appropriately Tarquinius' words '*tace . . . vocem*' (ℓℓ.6–8).   3

(d)   How did Lucretia feel when she first saw Tarquinius and what reason is given for her feelings?   3

(e)   How did Tarquinius at first try to persuade her (ℓℓ. 10–11)?   3

(f)   How did Lucretia react to these overtures?   2

(g)   What finally persuaded her to give way?   3

(h)   *expugnato decore muliebri* (ℓℓ. 16–17): what metaphor is used here? Which words earlier in the sentence lead up to this metaphor?   3

(i)   In this passage what qualities of character does Livy intend us to admire and condemn?   2

(j)   What part of speech is each of the following:
post (ℓ.1); *post* (ℓ.2); *postquam* (ℓ.4)?   3

(k)   In what case is each of the following words:
hospitale (ℓ.3); *mortua* (ℓ.13); *muliebri* (ℓ.17)?   3

Total 30

Hannibal crosses the Alps

In 218 B.C. Hannibal marched for Italy from Spain with an army of some
40,000 men and 37 elephants. The presence of Scipio's army and fleet on the
Mediterranean coast forced him to take the inland route over passes in the
Cottian Alps.

a. Encounter with mountain tribes

ubi agmen Poenorum in primos colles contendere coepit,
apparuerunt montani qui tumulos insederant. Hannibal suos
consistere, castra poni iussit; Gallisque ad explorandum
praemissis, certior factus est interdiu tantum obsideri
5   saltum, nocte montanos domum abire. itaque, simul ac sub
noctem barbaros custodias laxavisse sensit, multos ignes incendi
iussit; deinde, dum maior pars exercitus eodem loco manet, ipse cum
expeditis summa celeritate angustias evadit; tandem in iis ipsis
tumulis, quos hostes tenuerant, consedit. prima luce castra
10 mota sunt et agmen reliquum procedere coepit. iam montani
ad stationem solitam conveniebant, cum repente conspiciunt
alios hostes super caput esse, alios viam transire. primo
attoniti stabant; deinde, ubi agmen in angustiis maxime
turbari viderunt, decurrunt. tum vero quamquam simul ab
15 hostibus, simul ab iniquitate loci Poeni oppugnabantur,
Hannibal suos retinebat, ne tumultum augeret. postremo tamen,
postquam non solum exercitum sed etiam impedimenta vidit esse
in periculo, decurrit ex superiore loco et impetu hostes fugat.

Livy XXI, 32-3.

ℓ.1   *Poeni, -orum*: the Carthaginians.
ℓ.2   *insidere*: to occupy.   *tumulus, -i*: a small hill.
ℓ.4   *interdiu* (adv.): by day.   *tantum* (adv.): only.
ℓ.5   *saltus, -us*: mountain pass.   ℓ.6 *laxare*: to relax.
ℓ.8   *expediti, -orum* (m. pl.): light-armed troops.
       evadere, evasi: to pass through.
ℓ.11 *solitus -a -um*: usual, customary.   *repente*: suddenly.
ℓ.13 *attonitus -a -um*: astonished.
ℓ.15 *iniquitas, -atis* (f.): unevenness.
ℓ.16 *postremo*: finally.
ℓ.17 *impedimenta, -orum* (n. pl.): baggage, equipment.

(a) At what point did Hannibal's army meet opposition? What form did the opposition take? 3

(b) What orders did Hannibal give? 2

(c) What information did his Gallic scouts bring back? 2

(d) Lines 5—9 describe the trick Hannibal used to outwit the enemy: explain (i) exactly when he began to put his plan into effect; (ii) the point of *multos ignes incendi iussit* and (iii) the different parts played by *maior pars exercitus* and *ipse cum expeditis*. 6

(e) What did the enemy see next day that surprised them? Why did they nevertheless charge down? 3

(f) In what difficulties did the Carthaginians find themselves? 2

(g) *Hannibal suos retinebat* (ℓ.16): what was Hannibal's dilemma at this stage? 2

(h) What finally brought him into action? Describe the end of the incident from the enemy point of view. 4

(i) Explain the changes of tense in *tenuerant, consedit* (ℓ.9); *conveniebant . . . conspiciunt* (ℓ.11). Name the tense of each verb. 4

(j) Put down one verb from this passage that has been placed early in its clause, and explain Livy's intention clearly. 2

Total 30

b. Distress and encouragement

tandem nono die in iugum Alpium pervenerunt. saepe per
invia et errores iter Poeni faciebant, vel quod barbari duces
fallebant vel quod ipsi incerte viam coniectabant. biduum
in iugo castra habuerunt, fessisque labore ac pugnando quies
5   est data militibus; iumentaque aliquot, quae prolapsa in
rupibus erant, sequendo vestigia agminis in castra pervenerunt.
nivis etiam casus ingentem terrorem adiecit. signis prima
luce motis segniter per nivem agmen incedebat, pigritiaque et
desperatio in omnium vultu videbatur. itaque praegressus
10   Hannibal, consistere iussis militibus in promonturio quodam
unde longe ac late prospicere poterant, Italiam ostendit
subiectosque Alpinis montibus Circumpadanos campos. tunc
suis 'iam moenia' inquit 'transcenditis non Italiae modo
sed etiam urbis Romanae; cetera plana ac proclivia erunt; uno
15   aut altero proelio arcem et caput Italiae in manu ac potestate
habebitis.'

Livy XXI, 35.

ℓ.1   *iugum*: col, ridge.
ℓ.2   *invia* (n. pl.): trackless regions.
ℓ.3   *coniectare*: to guess.   *biduum* (adv.): for two days.
ℓ.5   *iumentum, -i* (n.): pack animal.
ℓ.7   *nix, nivis*: snow.   *adicere, adieci*: to add.
ℓ.8   *segniter*: sluggishly.   *incedere*: to advance.   *pigritia*: apathy.
ℓ.10 *promonturium, -i*: spur of a mountain.
ℓ.12 *subiectus -a -um* (+ dat.): lying below.
       Circumpadanus -a -um: around the river Po (in north Italy).
ℓ.14 *proclivis -e*: downhill.

(a) When did the Carthaginians arrive at the col? What had made the journey a long one? 4

(b) What did they do on the col? Why? 3

(c) What had happened to some of the animals? How did they rejoin the army? 2

(d) How did the weather then affect the army's morale? (𝓵.7). 2

(e) What signs of discouragement did they show as they set out at dawn? 2

(f) Where did Hannibal tell his soldiers to halt? Why was it a suitable place and what did he do there? 4

(g) What did he mean by his words '*iam . . . Romanae*' (𝓵𝓵.13–14)? How did he try to persuade his men that the final part of the invasion would be easy? 5

(h) Comment on Hannibal's qualities as a leader, as shown in this narrative. 2

(i) What part of the verb are: *pugnando* (𝓵.4); *praegressus* (𝓵.9); *erunt* (𝓵.14)? 3

(j) In what case are the following and why: *militibus* (𝓵.5); *vestigia* (𝓵.6); *casus* (𝓵.7)? 3

Total 30

c. A difficult descent

sed iter multo difficilius fuit quam in ascensu, quod
Alpes ab Italia, ut breviores, ita arrectiores sunt.
via enim praeceps, angusta, lubrica erat, ut nullo modo
sustinere se a lapsu possent, aliique super alios et iumenta
5   in homines caderent. venerunt deinde ad locum qui recenti
lapsu saxorum praeceps erat in mille pedum altitudinem.
Hannibal ubi nullam aliam viam esse cognovit, milites
praemisit qui per rupem iter munirent. primum, arboribus
circa deiectis, molem ingentem lignorum faciunt eamque
10   succendunt, ardentiaque saxa infuso aceto putrefaciunt. tum
rupem ferro pandunt et viam faciunt, adeo ut non iumenta
solum sed elephanti etiam deduci possent. inde in valles
inferiores descendunt; iumenta in pabulum missa sunt; quies
muniendo fessis militibus data est.

Livy XXI, 35-6.

ℓ.2   *ab Italia*: 'on the Italian side'.   *ut . . . ita*: just as . . . so.
      arrectus -a -um: steep, precipitous.
ℓℓ.3,6 *praeceps*: steep, sheer.
ℓ.4   *iumentum, -i*: pack animal.
ℓ.8   *munire*: to build (a road).   *rupes, -is*: crag, rock-face.
ℓ.9   *moles, -is* (f.): pile.   *ligna, -orum* (n. pl.): logs.
ℓ.10 *succendere*: to light a fire underneath.   *acetum, -i*: vinegar.
      putrefacere: to make friable, soften.
ℓ.11 *pandere*: to split, open up.
ℓ.13 *pabulum*: pasturage.

(a) Why was the journey down more difficult?   2

(b) Suppose you were one of Hannibal's army: describe the difficulties
     that you and others (including the animals) encountered (*ll*.3–5).   5

(c) What held them up at the next stage?   3

(d) How is Hannibal said to have solved the problem? (You may draw
     diagrams.) The operation had several stages, the last being *tum. . .
     faciunt* (*l*.11).   6

(e) How big did the *via* have to be?   1

(f) What relief did the lower slopes bring to different sections of the
     army?   3

(g) Give the case (adding singular or plural) and gender of the
     following adjectives: *difficilius* (*l*.1); *praeceps* (*l*.3); *recenti* (*l*.5).   3

(h) Give the precise meaning of *ut* in line 3.   1

(i) Explain the mood of *munirent* (*l*.8).   1
                                                                         _____
                                                                         Total 25

8 Three scenes from the life of Cicero

a. The young magistrate

Cicero's first official post was the quaestorship (quaestura) *at Lilybaeum in Sicily. In this passage he recounts an incident which occurred on his way back to Rome, when he visited the fashionable seaside resort of Puteoli on the bay of Naples.*

ego sic tum existimabam, nihil homines aliud Romae nisi de
quaestura mea loqui. omnibus enim eram visus in omni officio
diligentissimus: excogitati quidam erant a Siculis honores
in me inauditi. itaque hac spe decedebam, ut mihi populum
5   Romanum ultro omnia delaturum esse putarem. at ego cum
decedens e provincia Puteolos forte venissem diebus eis
cum plurimi et lautissimi in eis locis solent esse, concidi
paene, cum ex me quidam quaesiisset quo die Roma exissem et
num quid esset novi. cui cum respondissem me e provincia
10   decedere, 'etiam mehercule' inquit 'ut opinor, ex Africa.'
huic ego stomachans fastidiose 'immo ex Sicilia' inquam.
tum quidam, quasi qui omnia sciret, 'quid? tu nescis' inquit
'hunc quaestorem Syracusis fuisse?' quid multa? destiti
stomachari et me unum ex eis feci qui ad aquas venissent.

Cicero, pro Plancio 64.

ℓ.1   *tum*: i.e. 'when I was a quaestor in Sicily'.
ℓ.3   *excogitare*: to think up, invent.
ℓ.5   *ultro*: of their own accord, unasked.
     delaturum esse: deferre: to offer.
ℓ.7   *lautus -a -um*: smart, fashionable.
ℓ.10   *etiam mehercule*: yes, of course.
ℓ.11   *stomachari*: to become annoyed.   *immo*: no.
ℓ.12   *quasi qui*: like a man who . . .
ℓ.13   *quid multa?*: why (should I say) much? i.e. to cut a long story short.

(a) What did Cicero suppose was the main topic of conversation in Rome while he was in Sicily?   1

(b) Why did he suppose this?   3

(c) What hopes had he when he left Sicily?   2

(d) He arrived in Puteoli at the height of the season. How do you know this?   2

(e) What was he asked by a stranger in Puteoli?   2

(f) *concidi paene* (ℓℓ.7–8): translate idiomatically and explain why Cicero reacted like this.   2

(g) *stomachans* (ℓ.11): why was Cicero annoyed?   1

(h) *quasi qui omnia sciret* (ℓ.12); translate briefly and idiomatically.   1

(i) '*tu nescis . . . fuisse?*' (ℓℓ.12–13): had this speaker got it right?   2

(j) What does Cicero mean by *me unum . . . venissent* (ℓ.14)?   2

(k) What is Cicero's attitude to the way he behaved on this occasion? Could the passage be used as evidence that he was a conceited and humourless ass?   3

(l) Explain the use of the following cases: *Romae* (ℓ.1); *Puteolos* (ℓ.6); *novi* (ℓ.9); *hunc* (ℓ.13).   4

Total 25

b. His finest hour

In 63 B.C. Cicero was consul when Catiline attempted to overthrow the
government. Cicero received secret information of what was going on and
eventually had cast-iron evidence; for Catiline tried to persuade a Gallic
tribe to revolt and sent letters through Gallic ambassadors who were in Rome.
The leader of the ambassadors, Volturcius, informed Cicero and they were
arrested with the letters on them. The conspirators included several important
Roman citizens, notably the praetor, Lentulus.

quibus rebus confectis omnia propere per nuntios
consuli declarantur. at illum ingens cura atque
simul laetitia occupaverunt. nam laetabatur intellegens
coniuratione patefacta civitatem periculis ereptam
5   esse; anxius autem erat dubitans in maximo scelere
tantis civibus deprehensis quid facere deberet. tandem
confirmato animo vocari ad se iubet Lentulum, Cethegum,
Statilium, Gabinium, qui sine mora veniunt. consul
Lentulum, quod praetor erat, ipse manu tenens in
10 senatum perducit, reliquos cum custodibus in aedem
Concordiae venire iubet. eo senatum advocat Volturcium-
que cum legatis introducit. igitur perlectis litteris
senatus decernit ut abdicato magistratu Lentulus
itemque ceteri in liberis custodiis habeantur. interea
15 coniuratione patefacta homines plebeii, qui primo
cupidi novarum rerum fuerant, mutata mente Catilinae
consilia execrari, Ciceronem laudare coeperunt; veluti
ex servitute erepti gaudebant atque laetabantur.

Sallust, Catiline 46.

ℓ.4   *patefacere, -feci, -factum*: to reveal.
      eripere, eripui, ereptum: to rescue.
ℓℓ.10–11 *aedem Concordiae*: the temple of Concord was sometimes used
      for meetings of the Senate.
ℓ.14 *itemque*: and likewise.
ℓ.16 *res novae*: revolution.
ℓ.17 *execrari*: to curse.   *veluti*: as if.

(a) To what must *quibus rebus confectis* refer? 1

(b) Why was Cicero at once worried and cheered by the news? 4

(c) What order did he finally give? 2

(d) At the meeting of the Senate how did Cicero treat Lentulus differently from the other conspirators and why? 3

(e) *perlectis litteris* (ℓ.12): what letters are referred to and why were they read out? 2

(f) What decisions did the Senate make? 2

(g) How had the feelings of *homines plebeii* (ℓ.15) changed, and why? 3

(h) Cicero later looked back on these events as the greatest moments in his career. Suggest three reasons why he may have been proud of his conduct on this occasion, drawing your evidence from the passage. 3

(i) In what tenses are *declarantur* (ℓ.2); *occupaverunt* (ℓ.3); *laetabatur* (ℓ.3)? Account for the variation in tenses. 3

(j) Why is the subjunctive used in *deberet* (ℓ.6); *habeantur* (ℓ.14)? 2

Total 25

c. His death

*After the murder of Julius Caesar, Cicero in an attempt to save the Republic
rallied the Senate against Antony and denounced him in a series of speeches.
When Antony formed the Second Triumvirate with Octavian and Lepidus,
Cicero was outlawed and murdered.*

Cicero pro certo habens se non Antonio eripi posse,
primum in Tusculanum fugit, inde in Formianum ut
navem conscenderet proficiscitur. unde aliquoties in
altum provectus est sed, cum modo venti adversi
5   rettulissent, modo ipse iactationem navis ferre non
posset, taedium tandem et fugae et vitae eum cepit,
regressusque ad villam, 'moriar' inquit 'in patria
quam saepe servavi.' satis constat servos fortiter
fideliterque paratos fuisse ad pugnandum, sed ipsum
10 eos iussisse deponere lecticam et quietos pati quod
sors iniqua cogeret. prominenti ex lectica praebentique
immotam cervicem ei caput praecisum est. neque hoc
satis crudelitati militum fuit; manus quoque praeciderunt.
ita relatum est caput ad Antonium, iussuque eius
15 inter duas manus in rostris positum, ubi ille consul, ubi
saepe consularis, ubi eo ipse anno adversus Antonium
cum admiratione eloquentiae auditus fuerat.

Livy (fragment).

ℓ.2   *Tusculanum*: Cicero's estate at Tusculum, about fifteen miles south
of Rome.
Formianum: Cicero's estate at Formiae, on the coast about seventy
miles south of Rome.

ℓℓ.4–5   *modo . . . modo . . .* : at one time . . . at another time . . .

ℓ.5   *iactatio, -ionis*: tossing.

ℓ.6   *taedium*: weariness, disgust.

ℓ.8   *constat*: it is agreed.

ℓ.10   *lectica*: a litter, sedan chair.

ℓ.11   *sors, sortis* (f.): fate.   *prominēre*: to stick out.

ℓ.12   *cervix, cervicis* (f.): neck.

ℓ.15   *rostra* (n. pl.): the speakers' platform in the forum at Rome.

52

(a) What was Cicero's conviction when he fled to his Tusculan estate? 2

(b) He put to sea several times. Why did he return to land and what was his state of mind in the end? 4

(c) What did he say when he finally returned? 2

(d) How did his slaves feel when Antony's soldiers appeared? 2

(e) What did Cicero tell them to do? 3

(f) Describe his death. 3

(g) What did the soldiers do to him when he was dead? 1

(h) What did Antony do to Cicero's head and hands? What was the significance of this action? 3

(i) What is Livy's attitude to (i) the soldiers (ii) Cicero (quote your evidence)? 3

(j) To whom do the following pronouns refer:
eius (ℓ.14); *ille* (ℓ.15)? 2

Total 25

9 Three glimpses of Julius Caesar

The following passages show Julius Caesar first as a young man just embarking
on his career (77 B.C.), secondly at a crisis during his campaigns in Gaul
(57 B.C.), thirdly at his death (44 B.C.).

a. Caesar and the pirates

Julius Caesar iuvenis Cornelium Dolabellam consularem et
triumphalem repetundarum postulavit; absolutoque eo
Rhodum secedere constituit et ad vitandam invidiam et
ut per otium Apollonio Moloni clarissimo tunc dicendi
5   magistro operam daret. huc dum hibernis iam mensibus
navigat, circa Pharmacussam insulam a praedonibus
captus est mansitque apud eos non sine summa indignatione
prope quadraginta dies cum uno medico et cubiculariis
duobus; nam comites servosque reliquos initio statim
10 ad expediendas pecunias quibus redimeretur dimiserat.
numeratis deinde quadraginta talentis, expositus in
litore nihil moratus est sed statim classe deducta
praedones abeuntes persequebatur ac redactos in
potestatem supplicio, quod saepe illis minatus erat
15 inter iocum, adfecit. sed in ulciscendo se natura
lenissimum praebuit; nam iuraverat se praedones cruci
suffixurum esse, sed iugulari prius iussit, deinde suffigi.

Suetonius, *Divus Julius* 4 & 74.

ℓ.2   *triumphalis, -is*: a general who has held a triumph in Rome.
      repetundarum postulavit: prosecuted for extortion, i.e. for extorting
      money from provincials when governor of a province.
      absolvere, -solvi, -solutum: to acquit.
ℓ.3   *vitare*: to avoid.   *invidia*: unpopularity, hatred.
ℓ.5   *operam dare*: to attend to, study under.
ℓ.6   *praedo, praedonis* (m.): a pirate.   ℓ.8   *cubicularius, -i*: bodyguard.
ℓ.10 *expedire*: to fetch.   ℓ.11 *numerare*: to pay.
ℓ.14 *supplicium, -i*: punishment.   ℓ.16 *lenis -e*: gentle, merciful.
ℓℓ.16-17   *cruci suffigere*: to fix to a cross, to crucify.
ℓ.17 *iugulare*: to cut the throat.

(a) On what grounds could you say that Caesar was rash to prosecute Dolabella?   2

(b) Why did he go to Rhodes?   3

(c) At what time of year and where was he captured?   2

(d) How long was he in the hands of the pirates and how did he feel about his situation?   2

(e) Who shared his captivity and where were his other companions?   3

(f) When the ransom was paid (i) what did the pirates do with Caesar (ii) what did Caesar himself do?   1, 3

(g) How did he show mercy in taking revenge?   2

(h) What do you learn from the passage about Caesar's character?   3

(i) In what cases are *absoluto* (ℓ.2) and *Rhodum* (ℓ.3) and why are these cases used?   2

(j) In what mood is *redimeretur* (ℓ.10) and why is this mood used? 2

                                                        Total 25

b. The day he overcame the Nervii

By 57 B.C. Caesar had subdued central Gaul and was pressing north into Belgium. The most powerful of the Belgic tribes, the Nervii, attacked Caesar in full force while the army was pitching camp. The legions had to engage the enemy separately, while Caesar hurried from one legion to another organizing resistance. This passage describes the climax of the battle, which resulted in the virtual annihilation of the Nervii.

Caesar ab undecimae legionis cohortatione ad dextrum
cornu profectus est, ubi suos urgeri duodecimaeque
legionis milites confertos se ipsos ad pugnam impedire
vidit: omnibus fere centurionibus aut vulneratis aut
5   occisis, reliquos esse tardiores et nonnullos deserto
proelio excedere et tela vitare. itaque scuto militi
detracto, quod ipse sine scuto venerat, in primam aciem
processit centurionibusque nominatim appellatis
reliquos cohortatus milites signa inferre et manipulos
10 laxare iussit, quo facilius gladiis uti possent.
Caesaris adventu spe illata militibus, paullum hostium
impetus tardatus est. interim T. Labienus castris
hostium potitus et ex loco superiore quae res in
nostris castris gererentur conspicatus decimam legionem
15 subsidio nostris misit. horum adventu tanta rerum
commutatio est facta ut nostri etiam qui vulneribus
confecti procubuissent scutis innixi proelium
redintegrarent.

Caesar, de Bello Gallico II, 25–7.

ℓ.2   *urgēre*: to press hard.
ℓ.3   *confertus -a -um*: crowded.
ℓ.6   *scutum, -i* (n.): shield.   *militi*: from a soldier.
ℓℓ.9–10 *manipulos laxare*: to open up the maniples, i.e. to adopt a more open formation.
ℓ.13 *potiri* (+ abl.): to win control of.
ℓ.14 *conspicari*: to see.
ℓ.17 *innixus -a -um* (+ abl.): leaning on.
ℓ.18 *redintegrare*: to renew.

(a) What had Caesar been doing immediately before the events described in this passage? 1

(b) Describe what was happening to the twelfth legion. 5

(c) *scuto militi detracto* (ℓℓ.6–7): why did Caesar do this? 2

(d) What orders did Caesar give and what was the purpose of these orders? 2

(e) What was the result of Caesar's arrival? 2

(f) How did Labienus find out what was happening in the Roman camp and what did he do about it? 3

(g) What effect did the arrival of the tenth legion have? 3

(h) What qualities of generalship does Caesar show in this passage? 3

(i) *reliquos . . . vitare* (ℓℓ.5–6): what construction is here used, and why is it used? 2

(j) Quote from this passage (in abbreviated form) one example of (a) a final (purpose) clause (b) a consecutive clause. 2

Total 25

c. 'Then fall, Caesar'

Caesar was assassinated at a meeting of the Senate in the theatre of Pompey on the Ides (15th) of March 44 B.C.

Caesarem assidentem conspirati circumsteterunt, statimque
Cimber Tullius, qui primas partes susceperat, quasi aliquid
rogaturus, propius accessit et, cum renueret Caesar et gestu
in aliud tempus differret, ab utroque umero togam apprehendit;
5 deinde clamantem 'ista quidem vis est!' Casca aversum
vulnerat paullum infra iugulum. Caesar Cascae bracchium
arreptum graphio traiecit conatusque prosilire alio vulnere
tardatus est; utque animadvertit undique se strictis
10 pugionibus peti, toga caput obvolvit atque humum cecidit.
ita tribus et viginti plagis confossus est, uno modo ad
primum ictum gemitu edito; tradiderunt tamen quidam
eum Marco Bruto irruenti dixisse 'et tu, fili?'. exanimis
diffugientibus omnibus aliquamdiu iacuit, donec lecticae
15 impositum tres servi domum rettulerunt. nec in tot vulneribus,
ut Antistius medicus existimabat, letale ullum repertum est
nisi id quod in pectore acceperat.

Suetonius, *Divus Julius* 82.

ℓ.2 *quasi*: as if.
ℓ.3 *renuere*: to refuse.   *gestus, -us* (m.): a gesture.
ℓ.4 *differre*: to put off.
ℓ.6 *iugulum, -i* (n.): throat.
ℓ.7 *graphium, -i* (n.): a stilus, i.e. a pointed bronze instrument used for writing.
    prosilire: to leap forward. *traicere*: to stab
ℓ.10 *pugio, pugionis* (f.): a dagger.
ℓ.11 *plaga, -ae* (f.): a wound.   *modo* (adv.): only.
ℓ.12 *ictus, -us* (m.): a blow.   *gemitus, -us* (m.): a groan.
ℓ.13 *exanimis -e*: dead.
ℓ.14 *lectica, -ae* (f.): a litter.
ℓ.16 *letalis -e*: deadly, mortal.

58

(a) Summarize in about 35 words the events which are described
     between *Caesarem assidentem* (ℓ.1) and *iugulum* (ℓ.6). Include
     only what you would have seen if you had been present.   10

(b) How did Caesar attempt to defend himself?   2

(c) At what point did he give up hope and what did he do immediately
     before he fell?   3

(d) How many wounds did he receive and which one actually killed
     him according to Antistius?   3

(e) *'et tu, fili?'* (ℓ.13): what does this mean? Is it certain that Caesar
     actually said this?   3

(f) What happened after he was dead?   3

(g) What qualities of greatness did Caesar, in your view, show at his
     death?   3

(h) Distinguish the meanings of *aliquid* (ℓ.2); *aliud* (ℓ.4); *quidam* (ℓ.12).   3

                                                                     Total 30

10 Two uncomfortable experiences of the poet Horace

a. Journey down the Appian Way

This passage is part of a description of a journey which Horace made from Rome to Brindisi in the spring of 37 B.C. The total distance was about 375 miles and it took him 15 days. This passage covers the first 3 days, which took him from Rome to Aricia and Forum Appii by road (about 40 miles) and from there to Anxur by barge (linter) *towed by a mule* (mula) *(about 25 miles).*

Roma egressi illo die Ariciam advenimus ubi mansimus
in hospitio modico. inde Forum Appii processimus, plenum
nautis atque cauponibus malignis. hic ego propter aquam,
quae erat pessima, aeger factus sum et comites, qui cenabant,
5   anxio animo exspectabam. iam nox erat cum pueri nautis
et nautae pueris convicia ingerebant. dum aes exigitur,
dum mula religatur, tota abit hora. tandem linter procedit
sed mali culices ranaeque palustres avertunt somnum,
dum absentem amicam nauta ebrius atque viator certatim
10 cantabant. tandem fessus viator dormire incipit et nauta mulam
saxo religat stertitque supinus. iamque dies aderat cum
sensimus lintrem non procedere; tum viator cerebrosus prosilit
et mulae nautaeque caput latusque fuste verberat. tandem
quarta hora exponimur. tum pransi tria milia passuum repimus
15 atque advenimus Anxur, saxis late candentibus impositum.

                                      Horace, *Satires* I, v, 1–26.

ℓ.2   *hospitium, -i* (n.): an inn.
ℓ.3   *cauponibus malignis*: mean innkeepers.   ℓ.4   *aeger*: ill.
ℓ.5   *pueri*: the slaves.   ℓ.6 *convicia ingerere*: to hurl insults.
ℓ.6   *aes, aeris* (n.): bronze money (i.e. the fare).
ℓ.7   *religare*: to harness, tie up.
ℓ.8   *culices*: mosquitoes.   *ranae palustres*: marsh frogs.
ℓ.9   *ebrius -a -um*: drunk.   *viator*: traveller, passenger.
       certatim: in competition.
ℓ.11 *stertit supinus*: snores on his back.
ℓ.12 *cerebrosus -a -um*: hot tempered.   ℓ.13 *fustis, -is* (m.): a stick.
ℓ.14 *pransus -a -um*: after breakfasting.   *repere*: to crawl, travel slowly.
ℓ.15 *candens, candentis*: gleaming white.

(a)   In what kind of accommodation did Horace and his companions
      stay in Aricia?   1

(b)   Why did Horace not have any dinner the next night? What was his
      state of mind while his companions dined?   2

(c)   Describe Forum Appii, using the information supplied in lines 2–6. 3

(d)   What two activities took a whole hour?   2

(e)   Why couldn't Horace sleep during the journey (three reasons)?   4

(f)   What did the *viator* and the *nauta* do in the end (ℓℓ.10–11)?   3

(g)   When day broke, what did the passengers find?   1

(h)   What did the *cerebrosus viator* do?   2

(i)   How long, approximately, had the journey by barge taken?
      How do you know?   2

(j)   How far was Anxur from the place where they left the barge?
      Why could the barge not go the whole way to Anxur?   2

(k)   In what cases are *Roma* (ℓ.1), *Ariciam* (ℓ.1), *quarta hora* (ℓ.14)?
      Why are these cases used?   3

                                                              ─────────
                                                              Total 25

61

b. Horace meets a bore

ibam forte via Sacra, sicut meus est mos, nescioquid
meditans nugarum, totus in illis. accurrit quidam
notus mihi nomine tantum, arreptaque manu 'quid agis'
inquit, 'amice carissime?' ego 'bene' inquam 'et cupio
5   omnia quae vis.' cum me sequeretur, ego 'num quid vis?'
inquam. at ille 'volo' inquit 'amicus tibi fieri; docti
sumus.' ego 'propter hoc' inquam 'pluris mihi eris.'
misere discedere quaerens, modo celerius ibam, modo
aliquid in pueri aurem dicebam; at ille semper nugas
10   narrabat. cum ego nihil responderem, 'misere' inquit
'cupis abire; sed nihil agis. te persequar quo nunc
iter est tibi.' ego 'nolo' inquam 'te circumagere;
quemdam volo visere non tibi notum. trans Tiberim
procul cubat, prope Caesaris hortos.' ille 'nihil habeo'
15   inquit 'quod agam et non piger sum; usque sequar te.'

Horace, *Satires* I, ix, 1–19.

ℓ.1   *via Sacra*: this road went from the site of the Colosseum to the Speakers'
platform in the Forum.
     sicut: as.   *nescioquid nugarum*: some nonsense or other.
ℓ.2   *totus in*: absorbed in.
ℓ.3   *tantum*: only.   *quid agis?*: how are you?
ℓ.6   *doctus -a -um*: learned, cultured (often used of poets).
ℓ.7   *pluris mihi eris*: you will be worth more in my eyes.
ℓ.8   *modo ... modo ...* : now ... now ...
ℓ.9   *puer, pueri*: boy, slave.   *auris, -is*: ear.
ℓ.12 *circumagere*: to take out of the way.
ℓ.14 *cubare*: to be ill in bed.   *Caesaris hortos*: these were public gardens.
ℓ.15 *piger*: lazy.   *usque*: the whole way.

(a) What was Horace doing when the bore appeared? 3

(b) What was surprising about the way he greeted Horace? 3

(c) What did the bore say he wanted? What did he claim that he and Horace had in common? 2

(d) What is the tone of each of Horace's replies in lines 4—5 and 7? 2

(e) How did Horace try to get away from him? 2

(f) How did the bore come to realize what Horace was feeling? 1

(g) Translate *nihil agis* (ℓ.11). What does the bore say that he will do? 3

(h) Whom did Horace say he was visiting? Where? Why? 3

(i) How did the bore reply? 3

(j) In what case is each of the following:
nomine (ℓ.3); *amice* (ℓ.4); *ille* (ℓ.9)? 3

—————
Total 25

c. Horace and the bore (continued)

veneramus ad templum Vestae, quarta iam parte diei
praeterita, et casu tunc respondere vadato debebat;
nisi hoc fecisset, perdidisset litem. 'si me amas'
inquit 'paulum hic ades.' 'peream' inquam 'si aut
5 valeo stare aut novi civilia iura; et propero quo
scis.' 'dubius sum quid faciam' inquit 'utrum te
relinquam an rem.' ego 'me, sodes' inquam. at ille
'non faciam' et praecedere coepit. ego, quia durum
est contendere cum victore, sequor. sed, ecce, Fuscus
10 Aristius occurrit, carus mihi amicus, qui illum bene
noverat. consistimus. 'unde venis?' et 'quo is?'
rogamus et respondemus. ego vellere coepi, rogans eum
ut me eriperet. sed ille ridens simulavit se non
intellegere. fugit improbus et me sub cultro reliquit.
15 tum casu venit obvius illi adversarius et magna clamans
voce 'quo tu is, turpissime?' rapit eum in ius. sic me
servavit Apollo.

Horace, *Satires* I, ix, 35–78.

ℓ.2 *praeterire, -ii, -itum*: to pass (of time).   *casu*: by chance.
respondēre vadato: to appear in court on bail. The bore was involved
in a law suit (*lis, litis*) and had paid a sum guaranteeing that he would
appear in court to defend his case.
ℓ.4 *adesse*: to support someone in court (as witness to his good character etc.).
peream: 'may I perish', i.e. 'hang me, if . . .'
ℓ.5 *ius, iuris* (n.): law.
ℓ.7 *rem*: the matter, i.e. my case.   *sodes*: please.
ℓ.8 *praecedere*: to go ahead.   ℓ.9 *ecce*: look!
ℓ.12 *vellere*: to pinch, nudge.
ℓ.13 *eripere*: to rescue.
ℓ.14 *improbus*: 'the villain'.   *sub cultro*: under the knife.
ℓ.15 *obvius venire* (+ dat.): to come towards.
ℓ.17 *Apollo* was the patron god and guardian of poets.

64

(a) When did they reach the temple of Vesta?   1

(b) What would have happened if the bore had failed to appear in
court?   1

(c) What excuses did Horace give for refusing to support the bore
in court?   3

(d) What was the bore's dilemma?   2

(e) What did Horace suggest and what did the bore decide?   2

(f) Why did Horace follow him?   2

(g) What do you learn about Fuscus Aristius in lines 10–11?   2

(h) What did Horace and Aristius say to each other?   2

(i) Why did Horace nudge him?   2

(j) What did Aristius pretend and what did he do?   3

(k) How was Horace saved in the end?   2

(l) In this and the preceding passage how does Horace make his
description of such an annoying experience amusing?   3

Total 25

11 Mutiny in the Roman army

These passages describe the first of two simultaneous rebellions that broke
out among the legions in A.D. 14 on the death of the emperor Augustus
(whose chosen successor was Tiberius). Pannonia was a Danubian province
occupying roughly the area of modern Hungary. Blaesus was the commander
of the camp, in which three legions were brigaded together.

a. A rabble-rouser

tum tres Pannonicae legiones seditionem facere coeperunt.
Q. Iunius Blaesus, morte Augusti audita, munera laxaverat;
iam milites inertia et otio gaudebant. erat miles Percennius
quidam, qui pessimos ex militibus nocte ita adloquebatur:
5 'quam diu hanc servitutem passuri sumus? plus quam tricena
stipendia meremus, decem tantum in diem asses accipimus,
verbera centurionum, vulnera hostium toleramus. praetoriani
contra binos denarios accipiunt, post sedecim annos domum
redeunt et minus periculorum suscipiunt in urbe quam nos apud
10 horridas gentes. nonne tempus est novum principem precibus
vel armis adire?' haec furorem accendunt. magno clamore
tres aquilas legionum uno loco colligunt; simul exstruunt
tribunal conspicuum. interea Blaesus advenit multaque dicendi
arte persuasit eis ut legatos ad Tiberium mitterent. tandem
15 filius Blaesi Romam mittitur, et modica fit tranquillitas
inter milites, iam insolentiores quod legati filius causam
suam oraret.

Tacitus, *Annals* I, 16–19.

l.1   *seditio, -ionis* (f.): mutiny.   l.2   *munus, -eris* (n.): normal duty.
l.3   *otium, -i*: leisure, holiday.   l.5   *triceni -ae -a*: thirty.
l.6   *stipendium merēre*: to perform a year's military service.
      tantum (adv.): only.   *as, assis*: an *as* was worth one-sixteenth of
      a *denarius.*
l.7   *verber, -eris* (n.): whiplash.
      praetoriani (m. pl.): the Praetorian Guard, stationed at Rome.
l.8   *contra* (adv.): on the other hand.   *bini -ae -a*: two.
l.10 *princeps, -cipis*: emperor.   *preces, -um*: prayers, petitions.
l.12 *exstruere*: to build, pile up.   l.13   *tribunal, -alis* (n.): platform.
l.15 *modicus -a -um*: moderate.   l.16   *causam orare*: to plead a cause.
66

(a) Why were Blaesus' men in a cheerful mood after the announcement of Augustus' death?

2

(b) Show how Percennius chose a suitable time and audience for his speechmaking.

2

(c) What grievances concerned with length of service, pay, and working conditions does he mention?

4

(d) How did the legionaries' conditions compare with those of the Praetorian Guard?

3

(e) What action did Percennius recommend? What was the immediate effect of his speech?

4

(f) What do you think was the point of the soldiers' actions in lines 11–13?

3

(g) Translate *multa dicendi arte* (ℓℓ.13–14) (i) literally and (ii) idiomatically. What did Blaesus recommend them to do?

3

(h) Why did the men have reason to be grateful to Blaesus? What word in the Latin shows that they were not in fact grateful? Describe the atmosphere in the camp at this stage in the mutiny.

4

(i) What tense are the following and why:
adloquebatur (ℓ.4); *passuri sumus* (ℓ.5); *persuasit* (ℓ.14)?

3

(j) Account for the subjunctive mood in:
mitterent (ℓ.14); *oraret* (ℓ.17).

2

_____

Total 30

b. Clash with authority

The calm was not to last for long. An officer was insulted: Blaesus took action against those responsible but in a surge of sympathy the prison was broken open and the tribunes were attacked. The mutiny moved into its second, more serious stage, which is described in this passage.

ita redintegratur seditio. centurio Lucilius interficitur;
huic milites nomen Cedo Alteram dederant, quod cum vitem
fregerat in tergo militis 'alteram' clara voce et rursus 'aliam'
poscebat. his auditis Tiberius Drusum filium misit cum magno
5 comitatu; cui castris appropinquanti legiones obviam ierunt,
non insignia gerentes sed veste sordido vultuque maesto.
postquam vallum intravit, portas armatis confirmant atque
tribunal ingenti agmine circumveniunt. stabat Drusus silentium
manu poscens: tandem tumultu interrupto litteras patris
10 recitat. ubi tamen intellexerunt Drusum neque augere stipendia
neque labores adlevare in praesenti posse, clamore maximo
deserunt tribunal, castra pervagantur, manus intentant si
quibus amicorum Drusi occurrunt. unum ex his Cn. Lentulum
castris clam egredientem circumsistunt rogantes quo discederet:
15 simul ingruunt, saxa iaciunt. iamque lapidis ictu cruentus a
copiis Drusi servatus est.

Tacitus, *Annals* I, 23–7.

ℓ.1 *redintegrari*: to begin again.
ℓ.2 *cedo*: old Latin imperative meaning 'give me!'
     vitis, -is (f.): centurion's staff.
ℓ.5 *comitatus, -us* (m.): retinue.
ℓ.6 *insignia* (n. pl.): medals, decorations.   *maestus -a -um*: downcast, grim.
ℓ.10 *stipendia* (n. pl.): pay.
ℓ.11 *in praesenti*: immediately.   *adlevare*: to alleviate.
ℓ.12 *pervagari*: to roam through.
     manus intentare (+ dat.): to make violent gestures at.
ℓ.15 *ingruere*: to attack.   *cruentus -a -um*: bleeding.

(a) What happened to Lucilius? What was his nickname and how had he got it? 4

(b) What was the point of the legions' going out to meet Drusus? 2

(c) In what ways did their turnout not conform to the usual standards? 3

(d) How did they express their hostile attitude to Drusus once he was inside the camp? 3

(e) Why were they disappointed with Tiberius' letter? How did they express their discontent? 5

(f) Who was Lentulus? What was he trying to do? Describe the ugly situation in which he found himself, and his rescue. 6

(g) What is the difference between *alteram* and *aliam* (ℓ.3)? 2

(h) Account for the mood of:
fregerat (ℓ.3); *discederet* (ℓ.14). 2

(i) Why are these nouns in the ablative case:
agmine (ℓ.8); *tumultu* (ℓ.9); *castris* (ℓ.14)? 3

Total 30

c. Return to common sense

iam nox erat, et milites non solum minas sed etiam vim
apertam parare videbantur, cum subito luna claro in caelo
languescere coepit. hoc milites ignari omen acceperunt: nam
credebant si dea tenebris se celaret, res adversas significari;
5 si rursus fulgeret, omnia sibi prospera futura esse. igitur
strepitum tubarum cornuumque faciebant; luna tamen nubibus
condita est tamquam dei a sceleribus abhorrerent. itaque
Drusus ea fortuna usus nuntios iubet circumire tentoria:
'quam diu filium imperatoris obsidebitis? num Percennius et
10 Vibulenus stipendia vobis dare possunt? iam tempus est
paenitentiae.' paulatim mentes eorum commotae sunt: portas
non iam custodiunt, signa in suum locum referunt. primo
iussu Drusi Vibulenus et Percennius interfecti; deinde ceteri
seditionis auctores a cohortibus traditi sunt. tandem, dum
15 imbres saevi per multos dies cadunt et hos quoque caelestem
iram portendere illi credunt, constituunt castra relinquere
et in hiberna redire. Drusus, ubi omnia satis consedisse visa
sunt, in urbem rediit.

Tacitus, Annals I, 28–30.

l.1   *minae, -arum* (f. pl.): threats.
l.3   *languescere*: to grow dim.
l.5   *fulgēre*: to shine.
l.6   *strepitus, -us*: noise, din.
l.7   *condere, -didi, -ditum*: to bury, hide.   *tamquam* (+ subj.): as though.
    abhorrēre a: to shrink from, turn away from.
l.8   *tentorium, -i* (n.): tent.
l.10 *Vibulenus*: another ringleader.
l.11 *paulatim*: gradually.
l.15 *caelestis -e*: heavenly, of the gods.
l.16 *portendere*: to indicate.
l.17 *hiberna, -orum* (n. pl.): winter quarters.
    considere, -sedi: to settle down.

(a) What stage had the mutiny now reached? 2

(b) What was the *omen* (ℓ.3) and how did the soldiers interpret it?
Why does Tacitus call them *ignari*? 5

(c) What did they do to drive away the evil omen? 2

(d) Why did they think that their hopes were finally dashed? 2

(e) What points did Drusus' messengers make as they visited the men's
tents? 3

(f) Outline the steps taken (i) by the soldiers and (ii) by Drusus in
the general return to order (ℓℓ.11–14). 5

(g) What later occurred to increase the soldiers' feelings of guilt?
What did they eventually decide to do? 4

(h) Do you consider that luck or good judgement contributed more to
Drusus' successful handling of the situation? 3

(i) Account for the case of:
fortuna (ℓ.8); *vobis* (ℓ.10); *seditionis* (ℓ.14). 3

(j) Why is the infinitive *esse* used in line 5? 1

_____

Total 30

12   A good provincial governor

In July 51 B.C. Cicero arrived somewhat unwillingly in Cilicia (Southern Turkey), the province allotted to him by the Senate. It was in a poor state when he took it over; and the letters he wrote during his year of office reveal something not only of the provincial governor's duties but also of Cicero himself.

a. First impressions

Cicero has just arrived and snatches a moment to write to his friend Atticus.

CICERO ATTICO SAL.

consedi in ipsa via ut haec tibi scriberem. Appius
provinciam mihi tradidit vulneratam et semimortuam.
omnibus locis facta video non hominis sed saevi monstri.
aliae civitates gravissima tributa solvere non possunt;
5   aliae, quae locupletes sunt, magnas pecunias dabant ne in
hiberna milites acciperent. sed nunc levantur miserae
civitates, quod nullus fit sumptus in nos neque in legatos
neque in quaestorem: cum ad locum venimus, nihil praeter
quattuor lectos et tectum accipimus, vel etiam in tabernaculo
10   manemus. itaque concurritur ad nos ex agris, ex domibus,
ex omnibus locis. Appius, ubi audivit nos venire, in ultimam
provinciam se coniecit.

Cicero, ad Atticum V, 16.

SAL. (i.e. *salutem dat*): sends greetings to.
ℓ.1   *Appius*: the previous governor.
ℓ.2   *semimortuus -a -um*: half dead.
ℓ.4   *civitas, -atis* (f.): township.   *tributum solvere*: to pay tax.
ℓ.5   *locuples, -pletis*: rich.
ℓ.6   *levare*: to relieve.
ℓ.7   *sumptus, -us* (m.): expense.   *nos* refers to Cicero (plural for singular).
          legatus, -i: staff officer.
ℓ.8   *quaestor*: financial officer.   *praeter* (+ acc.): besides.
ℓ.9   *lectus, -i*: bed.   *tabernaculum, -i*: tent.
ℓ.10   *concurrere*: to run together.
ℓ.11   *ultimus -a -um*: the farthest part of.

(a) Explain *consedi in ipsa via* (ℓ.1). Why had Cicero done this?   2

(b) In what state had Appius handed over the province?   2

(c) To what does Cicero compare Appius?   1

(d) In what ways had the townships suffered under Appius' governorship?   4

(e) How many officials (Cicero included) were on his travelling staff? Identify these officials as far as possible.   3

(f) In what ways did Cicero avoid burdening the local people?   3

(g) What made him think that he was popular?   2

(h) What news had Appius received? What did he do? Suggest why Cicero uses the phrase *se coniecit* (ℓ.12).   3

(i) Account for the mood of *acciperent* (ℓ.6).   1

(j) Give the present infinitives of the verbs from which the following come: *tradidit* (ℓ.2); *fit* (ℓ.7).   2

(k) Explain the meaning of *concurritur ad nos* (ℓ.10).   2

Total 25

b. A second Alexander?

Cicero finds that he has to move swiftly against a threatened Parthian invasion of Cilicia. The Parthians were Rome's main enemy in the East and had defeated them two years earlier at Carrhae (53 B.C.).

CICERO ATTICO SAL.

Cybistrae certior factus sum Parthos Ciliciae imminere.
itaque sine mora iter in Ciliciam feci per Tauri pylas.
Tarsum veni a.d. iii Non. Octobr. inde ad montem Amanum
contendi, qui Syriam a Cilicia dividit, et qui plenus
5   erat hostium sempiternorum. hic a.d. ii Idus Octobr. magnum
numerum hostium occidimus. castella eorum cepimus,
incendimus; imperator appellatus sum. castra paucos dies
habuimus eadem quae contra Darium habuerat apud Issum
Alexander, imperator haud paullo melior quam aut tu aut
10   ego. ibi dies quinque morati, direpto et vastato Amano,
inde discessimus. rumore adventus nostri et Cassio, qui
intra Antiochiam tenebatur, animus accessit et Parthis
timor iniectus est. itaque eos cedentes ab oppido Cassius
insecutus est et ducem Parthorum occidit. erat in Syria
15   nostrum nomen in gratia.

Cicero, ad Atticum V, 20.

ℓ.1   *Cybistra*: for this and other places mentioned see the sketch-map opposite. Cybistra is outside Cilicia proper.   *imminēre* (+ dat.): to threaten.

ℓ.2   *pylae, -arum* (f. pl.): gates, mountain pass.

ℓℓ.3,5   In October the Nones fall on the 7th, the Ides on the 15th.

ℓ.5   *sempiternus -a -um*: permanent.

ℓ.7   *imperator*: to be saluted *imperator* by one's troops after a victory was a mark of distinction.

ℓ.8   Darius III, King of Persia, was defeated by Alexander the Great at the river Issus in 333 B.C.

ℓ.9   *paullo*: a little (adv.).

ℓ.10   *diripere, -ripui, -repum*: to plunder.

ℓ.11   Cassius, who later conspired with Brutus against Caesar, was governor of Syria, the capital of which was Antioch.

ℓ.12   *Cassio . . . animus accessit*: 'Cassius received fresh courage.'

ℓ.15   *in gratia esse*: to be popular.

(a) Why did Cicero leave Cybistra?   1

(b) What difficulties did he encounter at Mt. Amanus? What evidence is there that his campaign was successful?   4

(c) Why does Cicero find himself thinking of Alexander the Great? Does he consider Alexander to be a better or worse general than himself?   3

(d) What situation was Cassius in? How did the news of Cicero's arrival help him?   3

(e) From the information given, construct a diary of these events, with dates where possible.   5

(f) Cicero, a writer, politician, barrister, had never commanded an army in the field before. What is his attitude to his own exploits in Cilicia?   3

(g) Account for the cases of:
Cybistrae (ℓ. 1); *Tarsum* (ℓ.3); *Parthis* (ℓ.12).   3

(h) Account for the cases of these participles:
morati (ℓ.10); *direpto* (ℓ.10); *cedentes* (ℓ.13).   3

                              Total 25

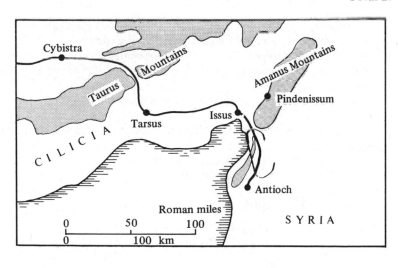

c. A successful siege

Cicero then had to deal with a hard core of resistance in a difficult part of Cilicia. He described the campaign in this letter to Marcus Cato.

M. CICERO IMP. S. D. M. CATONI

confectis his rebus, ad Pindenissum, oppidum Eleuthero-
cilicum, exercitum abduxi: quod est altissimus et munitiss-
imus locus et ab iis incolitur, qui ne regibus quidem
umquam paruerunt. ibi cives fugitivos recipiebant et
5 Parthorum adventum acerrime exspectabant. itaque propter
nomen imperii Romani constitui audaciam eorum comprimere.
Pindenissum vallo et fossa circumdedi, sex castella maxima
aedificavi, aggere, vineis, turribus oppugnavi, ususque
tormentis multis, multis sagittariis, magno labore meo,
10 septimo quinquagesimo die rem confeci. omnibus partibus
urbis deletis aut incensis, cives coacti sunt se dedere.
finitimi erant Tebarani, qui erant pari audacia: ab iis,
Pindenisso capto, obsides accepi; exercitum in hiberna
dimisi.

Cicero, ad Familiares XV, 4.

IMP(erator) was Cicero's new title (see the previous passage).
ℓ.1   *Eleutherocilices, -um*: the Cilician Freedom Fighters.
ℓ.4   *fugitivi, -orum*: refugees from the Amanus campaign.
ℓ.5   *Parthi, -orum*: for the expected Parthian invasion see the previous passage.
     acerrime: very eagerly.
ℓ.6   *nomen*: reputation, good name.   *comprimere*: to put a stop to.
ℓ.7   *castellum, -i*: fort.
ℓ.8   *vineae, -arum*: movable wicker shelters under which soldiers could move
     up to the walls.
     turres, -ium: movable towers for attacking walls.
ℓ.9   *tormenta, -orum* (n. pl.): siege artillery.
ℓ.10 *conficere, -feci*: to finish.
ℓ.12 *finitimus -a -um*: neighbouring.   *par*: equal.

(a) How did the position and past history of Pindenissum suggest that it might be difficult to overcome? — 3

(b) In what ways were its inhabitants collaborating with enemies of Rome? How does Cicero view this behaviour? — 3

(c) What was his motive for dealing with these people? — 1

(d) Write a description, or make a plan or sketch, of the Roman siege-works round the town. — 5

(e) Describe the final capture of the town. In what ways does Cicero imply that the siege had not been an easy one? — 5

(f) Who were the Tebarani and what effect did the capture of Pindenissum have upon them? — 2

(g) At what time of the year did this campaign take place? How do you know? — 1

(h) Does *quod* (ℓ.2) (i) refer to *oppidum* (ii) refer to *exercitum* (iii) mean 'because'? Explain your answer. — 2

(i) Distinguish the following uses of the ablative: *rebus* (ℓ.1); *die* (ℓ.10); *audacia* (ℓ.12). — 3

Total 25

13   A bad provincial governor

The following passages are taken from the speech in which Cicero prosecuted
Verres, who had been governor of Sicily. As governor he had been both commander of the Roman forces in Sicily and chief administrator of the law. In
both capacities he had to tour the province.

a. Verres tours his province

itinerum laborem, iudices, audite quam facilem sibi
Verres et iucundum reddiderit. primum temporibus hibernis
urbem Syracusas habitabat, ubi ita vivebat iste bonus
imperator ut eum non modo non extra tectum sed ne extra
5   lectum quidem quisquam viderit. cum autem ver esse
coeperat—cuius initium iste non a Favonio notabat
sed cum rosam viderat, tum ver incipere arbitrabatur—
dabat se labori atque itineribus; in quibus tam patientem
se praebebat et impigrum ut nemo umquam eum in
10   equo sedentem viderit. nam lectica octophoro ferebatur.
sic confecto intinere cum ad aliquod oppidum venerat,
eadem lectica in cubiculum ferebatur. eo veniebant
Siculorum magistratus, veniebant equites Romani.
controversiae secreto deferebantur, paulo post decreta
15   auferebantur. deinde ubi paulisper in cubiculo pretio
non aequitate iura discripserat, Veneri iam et Libero
reliquum tempus deberi arbitrabatur.

Cicero, II in Verrem V, 26.

ℓ.1   *iudices*: judges, i.e. the jury whom Cicero is addressing.
ℓ.2   *reddiderit*: *reddere* here = to make.
ℓ.5   *lectus, -i*: bed.   ℓ.6   *Favonius* :the west wind of spring.
ℓ.9   *impiger -gra -grum*: energetic.
ℓ.10   *lectica octophoro*: 'in a litter carried by eight men'.
ℓ.12   *cubiculum*: bedroom.
ℓ.14   *controversiae*: disputes.
ℓ.15   *pretio: pretium* = price (i.e. bribes).
ℓ.16   *iura discripserat*: 'had given judgement'.
          Libero: Liber is another name for Bacchus.

(a) How did Verres make the *itinerum labor* easy in winter?   3

(b) Why does Cicero call Verres *iste bonus imperator*?   2

(c) When did Verres reckon spring had begun?   1

(d) What was Verres' method of conveyance on his tours? Does this appear to have been the usual method for a Roman governor?   2

(e) Explain the reference of *eo* (ℓ.12).   1

(f) Who came to see Verres and why did they come?   2

(g) Describe how Verres settled disputes.   3

(h) Explain what is meant by *Veneri . . . arbitrabatur* (ℓℓ.16−17).   2

(i) What picture of Verres' character emerges from this passage?   3

(j) Cicero's chief weapon in attacking Verres here is ridicule. Give two examples of this and explain them.   4

(k) In what mood and tense is each of the following verbs and why: *reddiderit* (ℓ.2); *viderit* (ℓ.5)?   2

Total 25

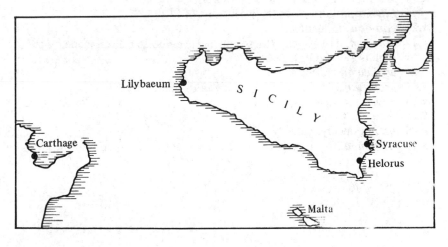

79

b. Verres the art collector

Melitensis Diodorus est, qui Lilybaei multos iam annos
habitat, homo et nobilis et gratiosus. Verres audivit
eum habere optima quaedam pocula summo artificio
facta. quod ubi audivit cupiditate inflammatus est
5   non solum inspiciendi sed etiam auferendi: Diodorum
ad se vocavit et ea poposcit. ille, qui sua servare
vellet, respondit se Lilybaei ea non habere sed Melitae
apud quemdam propinquum reliquisse. tum iste continuo
mittit homines certos Melitam qui ea quaerant. Diodorus
10   tamen ad propinquum suum scribit ut iis qui a Verre
venissent responderet se paucis ante diebus illud
argentum misisse Lilybaeum. ipse interea domo discedit.
quod ubi Verres audivit, adeo commotus est ut insanire
omnibus videretur. quia non potuerat eripere argentum
15   ipse Diodoro, erepta sibi pocula dicebat; minitari
coepit absenti Diodoro, vociferari palam, lacrimas
effundere. quaerere Diodorum per totam provinciam suos
iubet. ille tamen ex Sicilia iam discesserat et prope
triennium Verre praetore provincia domoque caruit.

Cicero, *II in Verrem* IV, 38–41.

l.1   *Melitensis*: a citizen of Malta (*Melita*).
      Lilybaeum: a town on the west coast of Sicily.
l.2   *gratiosus*: influential.
l.3   *poculum, -i* (n.): a cup (these cups were embossed silver, made by a
      famous silversmith).
      artificium: craftsmanship.
l.8   *propinquus, -i*: a relation.   *continuo*: immediately.
l.14 *eripere*: to steal.
l.15 *minitari*: to threaten.
l.16 *palam*: openly, publicly.
l.18 *triennium*: for three years.   *carere* (+ abl.): to be deprived of.

(a) What do you learn about Diodorus in the first sentence? 3

(b) What did Verres hear about Diodorus and what effect did this news have on him? 3

(c) How did Diodorus reply to Verres' demand? 2

(d) What did Diodorus say in his letter to his relative? 3

(e) How did Verres behave when he heard what Diodorus had done, and what did he say? 4

(f) What order did Verres then give? 1

(g) How did Diodorus avoid Verres' anger? 2

(h) Assuming that the story is true, what can you say about Verres' character? 3

(i) *qui . . . habitat* (ℓ.2); *qui . . . vellet* (ℓ.7); *qui . . . quaerant* (ℓ.9); *qui . . . venissent* (ℓ.11): account for the mood and tense of each of these verbs. 4

Total 25

c. Verres the commander-in-chief

unam illam noctem solam praedones ad Helorum morati,
cum fumantes adhuc nostras naves reliquissent, accedere
incipiunt Syracusas; nam quod saepe audiverant nihil
esse pulchrius quam Syracusarum moenia ac portus,
5   statuerunt se, si ea Verre praetore non vidissent,
numquam esse visuros. ac primo ad illa aestiva prae-
toris accedunt, ipsam illam ad partem litoris ubi
iste per eos dies tabernaculis positis castra luxuriae
collocaverat. quem locum postquam inanem invenerunt et
10   praetorem commovisse ex eo loco castra senserunt, statim
sine ullo metu in ipsum portum penetrare coeperunt
atque in urbis intimam partem; urbe enim portus ipse
cingitur. hic te praetore Heracleo pirata cum quattuor
parvis myoparonibus ad arbitrium suum navigavit. pro
15   di immortales! piraticus myoparo usque ad forum
Syracusanorum accessit, quo Carthaginiensium gloriosis-
simae classes multis bellis conatae numquam accedere
potuerunt. o spectaculum miserum ac acerbum!

Cicero, *II in Verrem* V, 37—8.

ℓ.1   *praedones*: pirates.
ℓ.2   *fumare*: to smoke.   *nostras naves*: i.e. the Roman fleet.
ℓ.5   *praetor*: governor.
ℓ.6   *aestiva (castra)*: summer camp.
ℓ.8   *iste*: that man, i.e. Verres.   *tabernaculum, -i* (n.): tent, pavilion.
ℓ.14   *myoparo, myoparonis*: brig.

(a)   What had the pirates done the day before the events described in this passage?   2

(b)   What did they do the next morning?   1

(c)   Why, according to Cicero, did they want to go to Syracuse?   3

(d)   Where did they first land and what did they find?   3

(e)   Where did they go next? How could they sail *in urbis intimam partem* (ℓ.12)?   2

(f)   How many ships were there in the pirate fleet?   1

(g)   How does Cicero make his indignation at these events plain? What is the point of the reference to the Carthaginian fleets?   4

(h)   Where in this passage does Cicero (i) raise a laugh at Verres' expense, (ii) imply that Verres enjoyed himself when he should have been on military duties, (iii) suggest that Verres was an incompetent coward?   4

(i)   Account for the cases of *noctem* (ℓ.1); *metu* (ℓ.11); *te praetore* (ℓ.13).   3

(j)   From the first sentence give an example of (i) a past participle (ii) a present participle, and say with which nouns they agree.   2

Total 25

14 The gladiatorial games

The pitting of man against man and man against beast in the amphitheatre
provided ancient Rome with its most popular form of entertainment. Most
Romans accepted the games quite uncritically; some even regarded them as
a quick means of reaping profit or popularity; others were not so sure of their
value in human terms.

a. An amphitheatre collapses

The following incident took place during the reign of Tiberius in A.D. 27 at
Fidenae, about five miles north of Rome.

Atilius quidam libertus amphitheatrum Fidenis aedificavit,
quo spectaculum gladiatorum celebraret. neque tamen fundamenta
in saxo solido locavit, neque firmis nexibus superiorem partem
coniunxit, quod opus susceperat non abundantia pecuniae nec
5 municipali ambitione, sed ut sordidam mercedem quaereret.
convenerunt viri et mulieres omnis aetatis ad locum, cum haud
procul esset Roma, avidi spectaculi quod tam diu a Tiberio
prohibitum erat. tum magno fragore aedificium collapsum quin-
quaginta milia hominum spectaculo intentorum vel debilitavit
10 vel obtrivit. postea senatus decrevit ne quis gladiatorum munus
ederet cui minor res esset quam H̄S̄ CCCC, neve amphitheatrum
aedificaretur nisi fundamenta satis spectata essent. Atilius
in exilium actus est.

Tacitus, Annals IV, 62–3.

ℓ.1   *libertus*: freedman, ex-slave.
ℓ.3   *nexus,-us*: cross-beam.
ℓ.4   *suscipere, suscepi*: to undertake.
ℓ.5   *municipali ambitione*: 'for the sake of popularity with his fellow-townsmen'.
      merces,-edis (f.): profit, gain.
ℓ.8   *fragor,-oris* (m.): crash.
ℓ.9   *debilitare*: to injure, cripple.
ℓ.10   *obterere, obtrivi*: to crush to death.   *munus,-eris* (n.): show.
ℓ.11   *res, rei* (f.): wealth, income.   *H̄S̄ CCCC*: 400,000 sesterces.
      neve (+ subj.): and that . . . not.

(a)   For what reasons was the amphitheatre at Fidenae unsafe?   4

(b)   What was Atilius' motive for building the amphitheatre? What word does Tacitus use to show his disapproval?   2

(c)   Who came to Fidenae on this occasion? Why did so many come?   4

(d)   Write a description of the amphitheatre's collapse based on lines 8–10, from the standpoint of an imaginary spectator who escaped death.   6

(e)   Anyone building an amphitheatre or giving a show after this tragedy had to fulfil certain conditions: what were they?   4

(f)   What are we told in this passage about Atilius' social status, bank-balance, and punishment? Quote the relevant Latin.   4

(g)   Why is the subjunctive mood used in *celebraret* (ℓ.2); *esset* (ℓ.11)?   2

(h)   Explain the different uses of the ablative in *Fidenis* (ℓ.1); *nexibus* (ℓ.3); *abundantia* (ℓ.4); *fragore* (ℓ.8).   4

Total 30

b. Cicero the spectator

Cicero had recently attended the games and shows given by Pompey on the occasion of the dedication of the Theatre of Pompey in 55 B.C. He is writing to his friend Marius who had not been there.

M. CICERO S. D. M. MARIO

quid tibi de ludis dicam? scaenicis non delectabar: quomodo
enim delectare possunt sescenti muli in 'Clytemnestra'
aut in 'Equo Troiano' tria milia craterarum aut arma diversa
peditatus et equitatus in aliqua pugna? haec omnia populi
5   admirationem excitabant; sed tibi, si adfuisses, delectationem
nullam attulissent. reliquae sunt venationes ferarum per dies
quinque, magnificae − nemo negat − sed quomodo potest homo
politus delectari cum aut homo imbecillus a validissima bestia
laniatur aut praeclara bestia venabulo transfigitur? extremus
10 elephantorum dies fuit, in quo admiratio magna erat turbae,
at nulla delectatio. etiam misericordiam populus habebat,
quod credebat elephantos quandam habere societatem cum
genere humano.

Cicero, *ad Familiares* VIII, 1.

ℓ.1   *scaenici, -orum* (m. pl.): theatrical shows, plays.
      delectare: to delight;   *delectari* (+ abl.): to enjoy.
ℓ.2   *sescenti*: innumerable (literally, 'six hundred').
ℓ.3   *cratera, -ae* (f.): wine-bowl.
ℓ.5   *admiratio, -ionis* (f.): wonder, amazement.
      delectatio, -ionis (f.): delight, enjoyment.
ℓ.6   *venationes ferarum*: 'wild beast hunts'.
ℓ.8   *politus -a -um*: educated, refined.   *bestia, -ae*: wild beast.
      imbecillus -a -um: weak, feeble.
ℓ.9   *laniare*: to tear in pieces.   *venabulum, -i*: hunting spear.
ℓ.11 *misericordia, -ae*: pity, compassion.
ℓ.12 *societas, -atis* (f.): common bond, kinship.

(a) From lines 1–4 (*scaenicis . . . pugna*) describe what Cicero saw. 4

(b) What did the remainder of the *ludi* consist of? How long did they go on for? 1

(c) In lines 6–9 (*reliquae . . . transfigitur*) Cicero both praises and condemns the wild beast hunts. Why? What happened in them? 5

(d) On which day did the elephant hunts take place? 1

(e) What were the conflicting feelings of the crowd toward the elephants? How does Cicero explain this? 4

(f) A more detailed account of these elephant hunts is given by Pliny the Elder in his *Natural Histories* (VIII, 20):

> *adeo populus dolebat, ut flens universus surgeret, dirasque res Pompeio imprecaretur.*

How does Pliny's description compare with Cicero's? 3

(g) Summarize Cicero's attitude to the entertainments as a whole and compare it with that of the *populus*. What attitude does Cicero attribute to Marius, and what would your own have been? 6

(h) Give two possible translations of *quid . . . dicam?* (ℓ.1). 2

(i) How do the tense and mood of the verb *adfuisses* make it clear that Marius was not at the games? 2

(j) Give two examples from the passage of words placed early in the sentence to give them emphasis. 2

_____

Total 30

c. Conversion to violence

Saint Augustine, writing of his Christian friend Alypius' earlier life, describes an incident that happened when Alypius went to Rome to study law in about A.D. 383.

ibi Alypius gladiatorii spectaculi cupidine incredibili
abreptus est. nam quidam condiscipulorum eum
vehementer resistentem (quia detestabatur talia) in amphitheatrum adduxerunt, ut crudeles ludos secum spectaret.
5   qui ubi consedit, oculos clausit ne in immanes voluptates
vulgi incideret. utinam et aures interclusisset! nam ubi
alter e gladiatoribus cecidit et clamor ingens totius
populi ortus est, ille curiositate victus oculos aperuit
et percussus est graviore vulnere in anima quam ille
10   gladiator acceperat in corpore. ut enim vidit sanguinem,
saevitatem quandam simul imbibit; et non se avertit,
sed fixit oculos, et delectabatur scelere certaminis, et
cruenta voluptate inebriabatur. quid plura? spectavit,
clamavit, exarsit. postea redibat non tantum cum illis
15   a quibus primo abstractus est, sed etiam alios secum
trahens.

Saint Augustine, Confessions VI, 8.

ℓ.2   *condiscipulus, -i*: fellow student.
ℓ.5   *immanis -e*: inhuman.
ℓ.13 *cruentus -a -um*: bloody.   *quid plura?*: 'need I say more?'
ℓ.14 *exardescere, exarsi*: to be on fire.

(a) How did it come about that Alypius visited the amphitheatre? Why was he unwilling to go?   3

(b) What did he do when he sat down and why?   2

(c) What did he hear and what effect did it have on him?   4

(d) What comparison does Augustine use to underline the seriousness of what was happening to Alypius?   2

(e) What was it that really 'hooked' Alypius? Describe the stages he passed through (*et non . . . inebriabatur*, ℓℓ.11–13).   4

(f) How did Alypius then show that he was thoroughly converted to the spectacle?   3

(g) Was this just a passing phase?   2

(h) Quote and translate two phrases that reveal the writer's own attitude to the games. Would you have shared his attitude or not?   3

(i) Quote two verbs that are used metaphorically in this passage and explain the metaphors.   3

(j) Translate *utinam et aures interclusisset!* (ℓ.6) and comment on the mood of the verb.   2

(k) Explain the different usages of *ut* (ℓℓ.4 and 10).   2

                                                Total 30

15 The murder of Agrippina

In A.D. 59 the emperor Nero committed what was, for Tacitus and perhaps
for later generations, the most notorious of his crimes—the murder of his own
mother Agrippina.

a. Debate

tandem Nero, quod Agrippina nimis odiosa fieret,
interficere constituit; dubitabat tamen, utrum veneno
uteretur an ferro vel qua alia vi. placuitque primum
venenum: sed inter epulas principis si daretur, ad casum
5 referri non poterat, cum Britannicus tali iam exitio
periisset. et servos Agrippinae corrumpere difficile
videbatur, quod mulier tam experta erat sceleris ut ad
insidias semper intenta esset; atque ipsa, praesumptis
remediis, muniverat corpus. ferrum et caedes quonam modo
10 celari posset, nemo sciebat; et metuebat ne quis illi tanto
sceleri delectus iussa sperneret. offert consilium Anicetus
libertus, classi praefectus et pueritiae Neronis educator
ac mutuis odiis Agrippinae invisus: navem se componere
posse cuius pars collapsa in mare eam profunderet, nec
15 quemquam naufragium suspicaturum esse: nihil enim tam
capax esse fortuitorum quam mare.

Tacitus, *Annals* XIV, 3.

ℓ.3   *qua*: some.
ℓ.4   *epulae, -arum* (f. pl.): banquet.   *casus, -us*: chance.
ℓ.5   *referre ad*: to attribute to.
ℓ.6   *corrumpere*: to bribe.
ℓ.8   *intentus -a -um*: alert.
ℓ.9   *remedium*: antidote.
ℓ.11   *delectus*: chosen, selected.   *spernere*: to disobey, reject.
ℓ.13   *invisus -a -um* (+ dat.): hated by.
ℓ.15   *naufragium*: shipwreck.

(a)   What decision did Nero take? What was his motive?   2

(b)   To what extent did he hesitate and why?   3

(c)   In what way was the example of Britannicus relevant to Nero's problem?   3

(d)   Why might it be difficult to bribe Agrippina's servants?   2

(e)   What further factor ruled out the first possibility?   2

(f)   What two objections were fatal to the second possibility?   2

(g)   Note down the information given us about Anicetus, and show how suitable he appears as adviser and agent to Nero.   4

(h)   How does Anicetus offer to solve Nero's problem? What are the advantages of his plan?   4

(i)   What insights does this passage give us into the character of Agrippina?   3

(j)   Why is the subjunctive used in *fieret* (ℓ.1) and *sperneret* (ℓ.11)?   2

(k)   What meaning is added to the following words by their prefixes: *praesumptis* (ℓ.8); *praefectus* (ℓ.12); *profunderet* (ℓ.14)?   3

Total 30

b. Failure

noctem sideribus claram et placido mari quietam, quasi
ad scelus convincendum, dii praebuere. nec multum erat
progressa navis, duobus e numero familiarium Agrippinam
comitantibus, quorum Crepereius haud procul a gubernaculis
5   adstabat, Acerronia super pedes eius cubitantis iacebat, cum
dato signo ruit tectum loci, multo plumbo grave, oppressusque
Crepereius et statim exanimatus est: Agrippina et Acerronia
parietibus, qui forte validissimi erant, protectae sunt.
omnibus turbatis, ei qui conscii erant constituebant unum
10 in latus inclinare et ita navem submergere; ceteri tamen
sceleris ignari contra nitebantur. verum Acerronia, dum
imprudenter clamat se Agrippinam esse utque subveniretur matri
principis orat, contis et remis conficitur; Agrippina silens eoque
minus adgnita (unum tamen vulnus umero excepit) in aquam se
15 iecit; mox nando occurrit lenunculis et ad villam suam
infertur.

Tacitus, *Annals* XIV, 5.

ℓ.2   *convincere*: to expose.   *praebēre, praebui*: to provide.
ℓ.4   *gubernacula, -orum* (n. pl.): steering oars, helm.
ℓ.5   *cubitare*: to recline.
ℓ.6   *ruere, rui*: to fall in, collapse.   *plumbum, -i*: lead.
ℓ.7   *exanimari*: to die.
ℓ.8   *paries, -ietis* (m.): wall (of room or compartment).
ℓ.9   *conscius -a -um*: accomplice, in the plot.
ℓ.11 *verum* (adv.): but.
ℓ.13 *contus, -i*: boat-hook.   *eo*: for this reason.
ℓ.14 *adgnitus -a -um*: recognized.
ℓ.15 *lenunculus, -i*: small boat.

(a) How does Tacitus describe the weather conditions? What comment does he add?   4

(b) Whereabouts on the ship were Agrippina and her two companions? Do you think they were anticipating any danger (give your evidence)?   4

(c) What was the murderers' plan? Why did it not work?   3

(d) What did they then try to do? Why were they unlucky not to succeed?   4

(e) Why is the adverb *imprudenter* (ℓ.12) used of Acerronia's actions? Do you think she deserves this description? What happened to her?   5

(f) How did Agrippina escape? Was she unharmed?   4

(g) What part of what verb is each of the following, and why is it used: *convincendum* (ℓ.2); *praebuere* (ℓ.2); *subveriretur* (ℓ.12)?   3

(h) Account for the following cases: *cubitantis* (ℓ.5); *grave* (ℓ.6); *matri* (ℓ.12).   3

Total 30

c. Success

The final scene occurred a few days later while Agrippina was recovering from illness at her villa.

Anicetus villam armatis circumdat, refractaque ianua
servos obviam euntes abripit, donec ad fores cubiculi
veniret; hic pauci adstabant, ceteris terrore inrumpentium
exterritis. cubiculo modicum lumen inerat et ancillarum
5   una; magis et magis anxia Agrippina erat quod nemo a filio
venisset ac ne Agerinus quidem; nunc solitudinem ac
repentinos strepitus extremi mali indicia esse. deinde
abeunte ancilla 'tu quoque me deseris' prolocuta, respicit
Anicetum trierarcho et centurione comitatum. 'si ad
10   visendum venistis,' inquit, 'filio nuntiate mihi bene esse;
sin ut scelus perficiatis, non credo a filio imperatum
fuisse parricidium.' circumsistunt lectum percussores et
prior trierarchus fusti caput eius adflixit. iam in mortem
centurioni ferrum destringenti protendens uterum 'ventrem
feri!' exclamavit multisque vulneribus confecta est.

Tacitus, Annals XIV, 8.

ℓ.1   *ianua, -ae*: front door.
ℓ.2   *abripere*: to arrest.   *fores*: doors of a room.
ℓ.4   *modicus -a -um*: quite small.
ℓ.6   *Agerinus*: an ex-slave whom Agrippina had sent to Nero to tell him of her lucky escape from drowning.
ℓ.7   *repentinus -a -um*: sudden.   *indicia* (n. pl.): evidence.
ℓ.9   *trierarchus, -i*: ship's captain.
ℓ.11   *sin*: but if.
ℓ.12   *parricidium*: murder of a parent.   *percussor, -oris*: assassin.
ℓ.13   *fustis*, abl. *fusti*: club.
ℓ.14   *destringere*: to draw (a sword).   *uterus, -i*: womb, stomach.
ℓ.15   *ferio, -ire*: to strike.

(a) Describe Anicetus' actions as he took over Agrippina's house. What happened to all except one of her servants?   4

(b) Where was Agrippina? What was her state of mind, and why?   3

(c) Explain *solitudinem* (ℓ.6) and *repentinos strepitus* (ℓ.7). How did Agrippina interpret the situation?   3

(d) To whom does she address her words in lines 9–12? What alternative explanations of their arrival occur to her?   3

(e) What is the point of her words *'non credo . . . parricidium'* (ℓℓ.11–12)?   2

(f) What is the significance of Agrippina's final gesture and utterance?   3

(g) What details indicate the determination and brutality of the assassins in the last section of the passage?   3

(h) Give two examples from the passage (other than those noted in the previous question) where Tacitus uses small details to increase the vividness of the narrative or to heighten its drama.   2

(i) (For those who have studied all three passages.) How does the reader's attitude towards Agrippina develop through this set of passages?   3

(j) To whom do the following participles refer? Explain the case of each: *inrumpentium* (ℓ.3); *prolocuta* (ℓ.8); *comitatum* (ℓ.9).   3

(k) Account for the infinitive *esse* in line 7.   1

_____

Total 30

Note to the student

The following suggestions are intended to help you with the comprehension exercises:

1. The passage should be understood as a whole before any questions are answered. It should be read through carefully at least three times: you will understand better at each reading. A glance at the title, at the vocabulary help, and at the questions may enable you to follow parts of the story which you have found difficult at first reading.

2. Before answering any questions, read them *all* and see how each question is related to the Latin. Look at the marks assigned to each question: these will tell you how full and detailed an answer is required.

3. Make sure that your answers are in good English and that they make sense and are consistent with the story as a whole. A non-sense answer is certainly wrong. Most of the questions require, not a literal translation, but a sentence or two to show that you have grasped the precise point at issue. A one-word 'Yes' or 'No' answer is never sufficient: one or more reasons must be added.

4. In answering the grammar questions make sure you understand exactly how the words concerned fit into the sentence; it is not enough simply to look at the word-ending. An accurate translation of the phrase concerned is often sufficient to show that you have understood the grammar.